I0190268

Understanding Bible Symbols

Understanding Bible Symbols

by Mark Heaney

2011

Creative Commons License

Understanding Bible Symbols by Mark Heaney is licensed under a Creative Commons Attribution-Non-Commercial-NoDerivs 3.0 Unported License.

Contents

INTRODUCTION 7

THE REAL STORY 48

SIN 60

NAKEDNESS 64

RELATIONSHIPS 66

BAPTISM 80

HEAVEN, HELL & WORLD 84

EGYPT, ASSYRIA, BABYLON & ISRAEL 87

POTTER 91

SEA & ISLANDS 94

TIME 96

CLOUDS 98

DESERT 100

THE SHADOW SHOWS 102

THE PLAYERS 107

DESTINY 175

BELIEVERS IN THE WORLD 181

UNDERSTANDING BIBLE SYMBOLS

By

MARK HEANEY

Introduction

Chapter One

Y DESIRE IN WRITING THIS book is to help those people that are sincerely trying to come to the knowledge of the truth regarding God, and his revealed Son, Jesus Christ, as they are revealed in the Holy Bible.

I believe that the Bible today is *exactly* what God wants it to be, and in the Bible we have everything we need to come to the knowledge of spiritual truth. I also believe that the only reliable source of information concerning God, and his plan, is the Holy Bible. The words of the Bible, every one of them, come directly from the Spirit of God. I further understand that the translators of the Holy Scriptures have been moved by the Spirit of the Lord to give us inspired translations of the Scriptures.

I am a Spirit gifted teacher of the Bible, and by that I mean, that the things that I can reveal to you I have myself received from God. I have never been formally taught concerning the Bible or about God. I have received my spiritual education simply by reading and believing the Bible. Everything that I have to say comes directly from the Bible, and points right back to the Bible. I am a Bible man. I like that name for myself over the name Christian, because the name Christian has be so poorly applied that it has lost almost all real meaning. The name Christian is a fine name as it applied to the first century believers that recognized themselves as little anointed ones, or little christs which is what the name Christian means. I too am a little anointed one, but to avoid confusion I

call myself a Bible man.

Within the text of this book I will quote many Scriptures. Usually right after or right before I make a spiritual statement. I have endeavored to show Scriptures for every point that I make. I want you, the reader, to see that the Bible is the foundation for every spiritual understanding. The Bible is the Rock on which we stand.

However, the fact that I support most statements with a Bible verse doesn't really mean anything. People are forever quoting Bible Scriptures to "support" all manner of incorrect ideas. Did you know that even Satan quoted Scriptures to support a wrong notion? [1] Almost everyone that has had anything to say about God has also incorrectly quoted Bible verses. So, what makes me any better than the others? Why should you believe my Scriptures and not theirs? Well, I am glad you asked. I don't want you to believe my Scriptures, or their Scriptures. The Bible is a complex book. The Bible is impossible to understand, unless God is with you—completely impossible. I want you to seek God in your heart and read the Bible, expecting God to reveal the Bible's true meaning to you.

Do you know what Biblical truth is? I ask you, which Bible verses are true? Is it the verses that you like? Is it the verses that you understand? Or, is it every single one? I know that you know that the last question was right. Every Bible verse is true. But, and this is a big BUT, that doesn't mean that every Bible verse is the Truth. I bet that statement gave you a double take. How can every Bible verse be true, but not the Truth? Well, I am glad you asked. The Truth is that which agrees with every Bible verse. I cannot take one brain cell from your body and then say that this is your body. I must take the whole of your cells as they are all together in bodily form and then say that that is your body.

When reading the Bible we cannot take this verse, and that verse, and some other verse, and then put them all together, and say that these verses make up a Truth. The Bible verses might indicate a Truth, but the real Truth, the whole Truth, is that which agrees with every verse in the Bible. This axiom is so true. God is not what you think he is. He is what he is. The Truth is not what you think it is, but it is what it is. When you consider some notion or other, you must consider that notion in the light of every Bible verse that there is. The whole Bible is the Truth. The whole Bible is God's revealed Truth.

Book, after book, after book, and sermon, after sermon, after sermon,

---

1) Matthew 4:5-7

will quote whatever Scriptures they may, but the Truth remains the whole Bible. So, when I, or anyone else, quotes a Bible verse to you, and says that it means this or that, you must consider the truth of the statement in the light of every Bible verse. What I am saying is, don't listen to me, go to the source and seek the Truth from God. Hear what I say, but then filter my words through the whole of Bible Scripture. What I am saying here is that you cannot read this book of mine and understand the Truth about God and his plan. You must receive your understanding from God, through the Bible. If you are not reading the Bible for yourself, then you are easy pickings for anyone that wants to persuade you. But, you say, I want to learn these Truths quickly and you say that you are a Bible teacher. Yes, I can help you to learn more quickly, because I am a Bible teacher, but you don't know that I am a Bible teacher. You don't know me from Adam. I could be wrong about most of what I talk about. The only way that you can know, is for you to have a personal relationship with God through the Bible, and be listening to the Truth, as it is revealed to you from God. Jesus said that his sheep could hear his voice.[2] So, listen to his voice; listen to the whole of the Bible. Let the Bible be your guide. Let the Bible reveal itself to you.

BEFORE I START I WANT to tell you a little bit about myself. My earthly father and mother divorced when I was about five years old. My mother was a Catholic and my father did not believe in God. My father was given custody of me and my two younger sisters and so we were raised as unbelievers. So, from when I was about five years old, until I left home at age eighteen, I was raised to believe that there was no God, and that anything to do with religion and or spiritualism was for ignorant and gullible people and/or for fools.

As an adolescent, and as a young man, I believed in science and in man's ability to solve his societal problems. More or less the vision expressed on the Star Trek television programs was my vision for mankind also. I then naïvely believed that man would learn the folly of racial prejudice, class superiority, national pride and everything else that divides us. I believed that man had already risen far above most of the problems of the past and would continue to rise until we had conquered the stars.

In my early twenties, I began noticing things that a spiritless existence couldn't explain. I started wondering, and looking around. I could sense something else, and so I began looking for what it might be. I didn't have a clue as to why I was even looking. It was just that it felt that something

---

2 John 10:27

was missing, and I wanted to know what it was.

Being born and raised in the United States, I was of course aware of Jesus Christ, but I really didn't know anything about him, beyond the fact that he lived about two thousand years ago and that he had reportedly preformed miracles and went about teaching people very cryptic things. I was also aware that he had been crucified on a cross and that after he had died that people claimed that he had come back to life. I was aware of this claim, but I didn't believe it to be true. The whole raised from the dead story seemed like an ancient tabloid headline to me. But, I was beginning to wonder what the truth about Jesus might be. It was all such a strange story. How could such a strange story persist for so long without there being something in it, I wondered?

During the same time of my life I also began to wonder about eastern philosophies, and about psychology and psychiatry, about Native American Indian ideologies and such. I wondered about the pyramids of Egypt and how they might have been built, and about why they had been built. I felt that there was more to life than science and the natural world, but I just couldn't figure out what it might be.

In college I had taken a class on the introduction to Aikido, which was a sort of philosophy class that was also physical. For that class I was supposed to read something spiritual and write a paper supporting some idea or other. I don't remember exactly what the point of my story was. I chose to read the Gospel of Matthew and so I read the whole thing and I didn't understand one word. That was the weirdest thing. I read the whole thing, and I knew all the words, and yet it was very weird. I did, somehow, manage to bend it into agreeing with my objective for the assignment, but I tell you, that book was very bizarre to me. I knew at the time that my spiritual idea for the paper was all wrong, but wow, what a strange book Matthew was.

Some years later, in 1977, I watched a television production that was/is called Jesus of Nazareth. It was six and a half hours long and was broadcast for three hours the Sunday before Easter and for three and a half hours on Easter Sunday. I watched it, and I was stunned, and I was astonished. When I had read Matthew I didn't understand pretty much anything, but while watching that video production I did understand the story.

While watching that biblical production, I was transformed into a person that believed that Jesus was, somehow, a special person, and that

he had the answers that I needed. I didn't know anything, but I knew that Jesus was no ordinary person, and that whatever being called the Son of God meant, I knew that he had some connection to God, and that it was totally important that I understood what that connection was/is. I didn't know it at the time, but I had been born-again while watching that show. Even though I didn't know much about Jesus Christ I believed in him.

I had to know more about Jesus Christ and I figured that I could find information about him in the Bible, so I went out and bought one of my own. I didn't know anything about the Bible beyond that it was an old book. But I did know that it talked about Jesus. So I gave Matthew another shot, but this time I wasn't trying to support any idea of mine, but instead I just wanted to know about Jesus Christ.

I read from Matthew to the end of John. What a strange book! I had never been much of a reader before this, but I really wanted to understand what this book, that is, what these Gospels were saying. What does it mean? How strange. I read all four Gospels and I didn't hardly understand anything, beyond that this was very strange stuff. Again, I understood the words alright, but this story was mega-weird, but I was starting to get an inkling of it.

I read the Gospels again, and again, and again, and again. I read for hours a day, day in and day out, month in and month out, for about a year or so. After maybe about six months or so I thought that I might also read the book of Acts. So I then included it in my cycle of reading. After some more time I noticed that Peter and John also wrote some letters in the New Testament and I figured that they were both with Jesus and so they could be trusted too. At some point I read some of Paul, but he was a persecutor of the Church and also his books were very hard for me to understand so at the time I stopped reading Paul.

After reading and reading for thereabouts three years or so, I was able to see that everything in the Bible, including Paul, was more or less reliable and important. I was beginning to be able to see that it all strangely fit together.

Somewhere in the middle of all of this I found out that my neighbors were church-going Christians, so I asked to go along with them one Sunday. I found that Christians were odd to me. They had the most exciting stuff in the world to be looking at, but none of them were excited about anything, and none of them could answer any of my questions, and I had a million questions, believe me. As far as I could tell, the Christians

that I had met had never really sat down and read their Bibles.

Some time later I was introduced to some other Christians that were of the Word of Faith movement. It seemed to me that they were as excited about the Bible as I was, so I hooked up with them and started going to their. They had a slew of books about faith and the power of walking in faith. Immediately I started reading as many of their faith books as I could get my hands on. They had dozens if not hundreds of books on faith and the Bible and I read most of them over the next few years.

At that time I was spending more time reading their books about the Bible and less time reading the actual Bible. I was getting confused and dismayed and I didn't know why. Things just weren't coming together. I had questions and I wanted answers. I KNEW Jesus was real, but everything was so messed up. They basically taught that if you had faith that God would move on your behalf, then God would, and you would be blessed. This sounded logical to me, and I had faith, but my life was one difficult thing after another. At the time I worked in a hospital and one day while going about my job I met one of my church brothers in the cardiac unit. He was embarrassed to be seen there by me, because of the whole faith and blessings from God thing. This bothered me a lot. None of this seemed right to me. Why should this guy be embarrassed to be ill? I mean, I knew why he was embarrassed, but it just wasn't right.

Some months later one night when I was at home, I was holding my Bible and I was praying, asking God what was wrong. I knew that I had faith; I believed in Jesus Christ, and so I was asking him why everything was so hard, and why I had so many problems in my life. As I was praying I sort of had a vision thing. It was sort of like a cartoon, or like a dream with cartoonish people; they didn't look real, but I knew who they were. I could see Jesus, (I knew that it was him, but it was not really him; I knew that the image I saw was supposed to be him.) Anyway, I saw myself standing beside him, holding his hand. He looked like a big father holding the hand of his small son, while we stood side by side. (Again, it didn't really look like me; I didn't look like anybody) but I nonetheless knew that it was me, and I knew that Jesus was there holding my hand. All of a sudden, Jesus started swinging me back and forth like a rag doll in a cartoon. Bang, bang, bang. Back and forth on my head, smash, smash, smash! From left to right, back and forth, back and forth, smash, smash, smash. This all looked like a Loony Tunes cartoon, but at the same time I knew that it was real and important.

I was shocked! I snapped out of this dreamy vision thing, and instantly became angry. I threw my Bible across the room, and I was real angry at Jesus. I didn't want any more to do with any of this. I was doing my best, and this is what I get? #$@%%!.

I didn't read the Bible or pray for about six months. All the while I knew that I was being an idiot and a fool, but what else was new. I was moving on. But things didn't feel right. Please understand that I was very young and very stupid. I still knew that Jesus was God's Son, and in fact I really knew this now, after having read the Bible for I don't know how many hundreds if not thousands of hours. I was angry that the Lord would do that to me, but what else was there? I knew that Jesus was the way, and that there was no other way. I knew this, but I didn't like it, but I did know it.

Anyway, I wanted to know what was going on with that first vision so I prayed again and I had a similar vision. It was cartoonish again, like the first one, but in this visual there was no action. I asked Jesus why he had been banging me back and forth, and I 'heard' Jesus tell me that he wasn't banging me back and forth. He told me that he was holding on to my hand and I was running off with every wrong idea or so-called understanding.

I asked him what I should do, and he told me to stop reading all of those books and read only the Bible. He then told me that if I would read the Bible he would reveal himself to me.

So I stopped reading everything about the Bible and once again started reading the actual Bible. Hour upon hour, day upon day, month upon month… It is now some twenty-five years or so later and I have learned a lot of things. I don't believe that I am a special person in any way. I also believe that what Jesus told me applies also to everyone. Read the Bible. Read the Bible and put into practice what you see. Trust in what you see in the Bible, and don't let other people pull you away from your personal relationship with Jesus, that you have through the Bible.

Some of what I have learned is that you don't need anything except the Bible, and your life to live it in. There are very few people out in the world that can tell you anything accurate and true about the Bible and/ or about God. I would say that you are pretty much on your own, except that you are not alone; God is with you and he alone is your Teacher. God will speak to you though the Bible, whether or not you think that you are understanding it. It doesn't matter if you understand what you are

reading; read. Read, and the understanding will come. Believe in Jesus Christ and believe also in yourself. Believe that when you do understand something in the Bible, that you do in fact understand it. People will try to pull you away from the Truth, but you must have faith in Jesus Christ, and in yourself, that is, in your ability to read and eventually understand.

Now, I believe that I do in fact know some things about the Bible, and I can point them out to you, but I am not your Teacher, and I cannot teach you anything. You must read the Bible for yourself and seek revelation of God, for yourself. I see myself as a pointer-outer-er. I can point things out and make connections for you that have taken me many years to make, and you can read them and keep them in mind and see if they make things clearer for you too.

The Bible is not an easy to understand book. I ask you, is it a surprise to you that a book that reveals God Almighty would at first be difficult to understand? God is a complex person. He behaves the way he behaves, and this because he understands what he understands. If you understood the things that God does, then you too would act much different than you do. When we first come to him we are very different than he is. We start out as ignoramuses. When we first come to him we are like newborn babes. As children it is natural to be self-centered, but as we mature we take on adult responsibilities, and through self-discipline we become more and more like him. This is not an automatic thing. We must respect our heavenly Father, and obey him in all the little things, as we grow and grow into godlike children of God. The Bible says that we were created in his image and after his likeness[3], so we can grow and mature into a person that is like God, in terms of understanding him and enjoying him, and in terms of becoming a person that God can enjoy to be around. We have it built into us to understand what sort of person God is. We have it built into us to become like God in our attitudes and interpersonal relationship with him. As much as your own child is like you, you can be like God.

I would like you to stop and think about what sort of adult would result from a boy or girl that was exclusively raised by wild animals from infancy. Would such a person grow up to be like other human adults? Clearly the answer is no. That person would end up so different than other humans that they could hardly be called human. Everything that such a person learned would be wrong in terms of humanity. This being completely true, then how can you possibly grow up to be like God if you are raised exclusively by humans? This is especially true if a person

3) Genesis 1:26-27

was raised by very ungodly parents, or in some society or other that knew nothing about God as he is revealed in the Bible.

The first step to spiritual maturity is to be raised by parents that know God, in a society that is ordered along godly principles and values. Then as you learn discipline from early childhood up through maturity, you then develop a personal relationship with God himself through the Bible. As God disciplines you, and reveals himself to you through the Bible you then grow into a spiritually mature person, a true child of God.

> **Luke 6:39–40**
> **He also told them this parable: "Can a blind man lead a blind man? Will they not both fall into a pit? 40 A student is not above his teacher, but everyone who is fully trained will be like his teacher. (NIV84)**

In this parable Jesus is telling us that we can never grow above our Teacher, that is, above God, but we can be like God. We can be like God, not in power and capacity, but like him in terms of the person that he is. We have the capacity for true fellowship with God. In my mind there is nothing more wonderful than that, or more important.

Now, I have just described an ideal situation, but seldom is one truly raised by parents that really know God. Seldom are things so ideal, but you nonetheless must grow past your upbringing and continue your spiritual growth by putting your focus on God, and reading the Bible with the intent to understand it and to walk in its ways.

You are not alone in this; God is active in revealing himself to you. You are no more alone in this than you were when you were five years old. Your spiritual Father has a far greater interest in you than your parents ever did. This might not seem to be the case, but it is nonetheless absolutely true. God is vested in your growth, to the point that he was willing to suffer and die for you. If that statement sounds like a cliché then you just haven't really thought about it. No parent of the earth has ever cared more for his or her child than God cares for you. However, God doesn't keep us against our own will, even when it is best for us. Man cut himself off from God through an act of direct rebellion in the Garden of Eden, and every child born from that man has been raised by their parents instead of by God. Think about this. Had man not sinned in the Garden every child would have been raised as Jesus was raised, with the Spirit of God inside of him or her. Because of man's spiritual separation from God, things are pretty royally messed up. But God has

not lost hope, nor has his given up; quite the contrary, God has from that day to this day, continued to reveal himself to man and has encouraged each and every man to come to him and walk in his ways. God is more revealed to man today than ever before if you are thinking of all men.

You, my friend, must break away from the ways of the earth, and by an act of your own sovereign will, seek God in the Scriptures and walk in his ways. You must do it. You can do it. You can always do the will of God for you.

After Jesus was resurrected we have such an advantage over all those that lived before. We, after being born-again, have the same Spirit of the Lord that was inside of Jesus, inside of us.[4]

What is it that you think God wants from you anyway? Do you think that God needs for you to worship him so as to bolster his ego? Is God a man that such foolishness would prevail? God does not need you to make him feel more powerful. God doesn't want followers so that he can be the boss of others, and neither does God want any pets. Such thinking is foolish thinking; it is the thinking of Satan. God wants to elevate you from being a little higher than the animals to being one with him. God's love for you is so great that he wants you to become his personal friend. Can you even imagine that; a friend of God; a child of God that is also a friend? To be a true friend of your parent, God, is to be a mature son or daughter of God.

IN THE FIRST PART OF this book I am going to talk about some of the general fundamental ideas and concepts that you must understand in order to understand the prophecies which will allow you to see the big picture. I believe that it is important to understand these before diving into the prophecies themselves. The prophecies are mostly written in symbolic language and have certain characteristics that must be first understood to understand the meaning of the prophecy. Much of the real information in the Bible's stories is found in the symbolic aspects of the stories. The nation of Egypt, for example, doesn't usually mean just Egypt, but rather, Egypt is usually symbolic for the whole world, and when you understand this and then read the references to Egypt, you can then see the big picture, that is you can see how the meaning affects the whole world and not just some ancient nation. This understanding transfers an historical story into a meaningful life-changing revelation about God and his worldwide plan.

It is my hope and my desire that I will be able to convey to you, my dear reader, what the Bible is for, and what God is going to do in the world.

4) John 14:15-17

God is working out a very specific plan, and the Bible reveals what that plan is, and why that plan is, and when that plan is, if you know how to read the Bible.

Reality

I AM NOT A RELIGIOUS PERSON. I don't care a hoot about religion, and I don't believe God does either. I believe in God. I believe in Jesus Christ. I believe in the Bible. I believe that spiritual reality is all around us, and that God, through the Bible, will reveal that reality to you and to me. The reality that God reveals is the real reality. The world's reality is the reality of a fallen existence. Those that focus their whole attention on the world's reality will never see past it into the reality of life, that is, into eternity. They will only see the reality of death, that is, separation from God.

Everything that a religion can do is only a shadow of the Truth. You might observe the shadow so that you can see the real. It is the real, however, that is truly important. God gave to the Jews many religious laws and observances, but these were only given to point the way to Jesus Christ, to a people that were unwilling to obey the spirit of the law. These laws and observances were a shadow of the reality that would come. And once Jesus came, the reality became so much more important than the shadow. Imagine, if you will, that you can see the shadow of your loved one coming to you. The shadow is exciting because it foretells the happy day of the loved one actually coming. But once the loved one arrives, who remembers the shadow?

Many people today worship the shadow and don't even believe in the reality. The shadow has been deformed into just what they want. But, the reality is standing at the door, knocking, asking you to open the door.[5] Open the door of your heart to the reality that is Christ Jesus. The Bible will clarify the shadow for you, so that you can recognize the truth when it is there before you.

I don't know about you, but for me, I would at least like to know what the truth is. I might not want to conform to the truth, but at least I know what it is. What good is it to believe a lie? What benefit does the comforting lie impart to you? Let's be real. Let's be strong, and look at reality, right in the face. Let us be able to make informed decisions, decisions that can save our lives.

---

5) Revelation 3:20

The Bible teaches you to see spiritual reality so that you can distinguish it from the world's reality. Once you can see it, you can then respond to it. Once you can see the reality, you are no longer just a wave blown along by the wind. Once you see the reality, you can become rooted to the Rock that neither the wind nor the waves can move. Once you see the reality, you can become part of that immovable rock too.

The New International Bible

IT IS MY OPINION THAT The New International Version Bible is an excellent modern English translation of both the Old Testament and the New Testament. I have read many other translations over the years and I have never found a translation that I believe is better or more accurately expresses what the Spirit of the Lord is saying. This is my opinion.

I am not a Bible translator and I have next to no knowledge of the original languages from which the translation was made. So my opinion is not based on any expert translation knowledge, but rather on my familiarity with the Spirit of God. Jesus said that his sheep will know his voice and I know that this is true with respect to me. When I read the New International Version, I have a sense of rightness. I can't explain it better than that. If you have a Bible that you like better, then by all means read that one. I know that the Spirit of the Lord can speak through any translation, and you should read whatever translation you feel is best.

Some years ago, I met a man and his wife that had very similar understanding of the Bible to me. I was very surprised to meet anyone else that understood subtle things in the Bible. I asked him how he came by this knowledge, and I found that he and his wife had done the same thing that I had done, that is, they read the Bible for hours every day for more than a year. I asked him which translation had he read and I was very surprised to hear that it was the Good News Bible. The Good News translation is really a paraphrase translation. I don't believe that it was translated from the original languages at all, but from other English translations. This surprise opened my eyes though. I understood that the Spirit of the Lord can use any translation to impart true understanding. My friends, however, did not have a good understanding of the Bible prophecies. I believe that understanding the prophecies requires the best of translations to become clear. The prophecies frequently use very specific wording to reveal certain connections within them. I will talk about these key phrases

later as we are looking at them.

One thing that Bible readers should be very careful about is that they should not read a whole bunch of translations at the same time looking for one that says what they want to hear. Nor do I think that non-expert Bible readers should put too much emphasis on Bible dictionaries and such. Most likely the people that translated your Bible into English were much more qualified to choose which English words to use to capture the most accurate meaning of the original languages. Too many times I have seen people piece together an idea from several translations which, in the end, is not what the Spirit was saying in the first place.

My advice in this matter is to pick a translation and then read it through. If you then wish to get a slightly different look at things then pick another translation and then read that one through. The Spirit can speak clearly to you through any translation, but the Spirit is the boss and not you.

The Lord God inspired the original writers to put down what the Lord wanted and he also inspired the modern Bible translators to translate the original texts into modern languages.

My Annotations

NOTE ON SOME NOTATIONS OF mine: If you see any square brackets [ ] within Bible passages they were added by me usually to make some point clear. Sometimes when Jesus is speaking I put his name there between the square brackets so that you can understand that he is the one speaking.

Also any italicized words within Bible passages are emphasis that I have added.

The Bible's Importance

HE BIBLE IS EVERYTHING. IT is not possible to overstate the Bible's importance to you personally and to each and every human on the planet. There is nothing on earth to compare it to. It is unique and is truly the most valuable thing on earth-now and for the entire history of man; that is, from Adam until that future man that is alive on the last day of planet Earth.

I love the Bible. It is the most interesting 'thing' in the world. I find it completely fascinating and captivating, from the smallest jot, to the

largest book; old and new, all of it.

The Bible, front to back, Old Testament through New Testament, is perfect just as it is. Through the Bible you can see the invisible Almighty God. That right there is enough to justify everything I have just said about it.

Imagine that you were given a magic mirror through which you could see into heaven and see God the Creator Himself. What would such a mirror be worth to you, or to anyone? Could you put a price on it? Could you really compare its value with anything else? Since we are really eternal spirit beings hidden inside of physical bodies, I think not. The Bible truly is such a mirror, but the way to activate it is by way of your mind and by way of your spirit. It does take 'magic powers' to see into this mirror, or rather I should say, supernatural powers, for the power to activate the Bible does not come from this creation but rather from God. I am clearly speaking figuratively here, using physical world words to describe spiritual things. It is God who calls to a person, and it is God who opens that person's eyes so that they can see. It is God who gives the understanding and makes the Bible come alive. You however also have a part in all of this. You must open your heart to God and look for him in truth. God speaks to us in a very tiny voice and we must quiet ourselves to hear.

> **1 Kings 19:11–13**
> **The LORD said, "Go out and stand on the mountain in the presence of the LORD, for the LORD is about to pass by."**
> **Then a great and powerful wind tore the mountains apart and shattered the rocks before the LORD, but the LORD was not in the wind. After the wind there was an earthquake, but the LORD was not in the earthquake. ¹²After the earthquake came a fire, but the LORD was not in the fire. And after the fire came a gentle whisper. ¹³When Elijah heard it, he pulled his cloak over his face and went out and stood at the mouth of the cave.**
> **Then a voice said to him, "What are you doing here, Elijah?" (NIV84)**

If you have your iPod pumping noise into your ears, and worldly images continually flashing before your eyes, how can you possibly hear and see the Lord? I'll tell you now that it will not be possible for you. You must make a decision, must make a choice. You must take charge of your eternal destiny and make yourself turn from the world and tread up the narrow road to God.

If you are so enamored with the world, and its glittery trinkets, that you ignore the subtle call of God, then just what do you think your eternal destiny will be? I am not saying that you should "find Jesus" in the traditional way; no, you must forget the world's way of doing everything, and read the Bible, and seek God on your own. The Bible is the key.

The Lord God Almighty cries out to you …

Matthew 11:28
"Come to me, all you who are weary and burdened, and I will give you rest. (NIV84)

Jesus offers to you spiritual rest and spiritual peace. He is offering to open your eyes, and to open your ears, so that you can both see and hear him, not physically but spiritually.

Jesus speaks to those that seek him …

Matthew 13:16–17
But blessed are your eyes because they see, and your ears because they hear. [17] For I tell you the truth, many prophets and righteous men longed to see what you see but did not see it, and to hear what you hear but did not hear it. (NIV84)

My friend, this book is about God's entire plan for you, personally, and about God's plan for mankind, and also the destiny of the angels. But I promise you that you will not understand one word of any of this if you are not right with God. Unless you are willing to die to the world and live for God, you will never have eyes that see nor ears that hear. There is nothing, and I mean nothing, that I can do about this.

If you are reading this hoping for a quick fix for your spiritual life then you will not get it. No one, and I mean no one, can tell you anything real about God. It is God that must open your eyes and ears. God is portrayed in the Bible as a man who is proposing a marriage-like union with those that will respond. We, respondents, are collectively the Bride of Christ. Now, I ask you, what sort of bride do you think God wants? For starters, he wants a bride that wants him. He wants a bride that loves him too, the real him, and not some idealized puppet of him that will put an okay stamp on whatever you want or think. He is who he is, and you must come to him.

If you really want to know the real God then you must find him in the Bible. The Gospels are a good place to start, but the Spirit of the Lord is in Genesis 1:1 through to the end of Revelation. God is the loving and protective hen that shelters her chicks under her wings and he is the

avenging King who marches through the blood of those who are ruining the world, smashing them to pieces with his iron scepter.

God is loving and kind, and he is awesome in his power and will consign the wicked to the eternal lake of burning fire. Should you be afraid of God? Yes. Should you love him too? Yes. He is complicated and he is simple too. God is who he is and that is that. You can shake your fist at him and condemn him in your eyes, but what do you really know about anything? Did you create heaven and earth? Do you know anything about justice? Do you really know what love is?

In this book I will be talking about most of the major steps in God's plan and what they mean. I am talking about what has happened in the past and what the prophecies say will happen in the future, but before I get into those things I believe that it is necessary to cover in some detail some of the basic understandings in the Bible. I don't believe that a person can understand the Bible prophecies without first knowing the Lord God Almighty better. What I mean is that I believe most people have seen enough of the Book of Revelation to have some idea about what is going to happen, but what people really need to know is why things are going to happen, and what it all means to them personally. I hope that if you are reading this that you don't jump ahead to the "good stuff" and skip the more fundamental things. Unless the building has a solid foundation, it will not stand long. I must build a foundation on which I can construct the Bible Scenario.

Religion

s *I SAID BEFORE, I* am not a religious person, and you might think it strange that I say this. People are always telling me that I am very religious, but what they mean is that I am focused on God. I don't believe that the Lord God Almighty is religious either. As I said before, religion is only a shadow of the truth. Shadows come before the reality. God's shadow came before he came. Before man was ready for the real, God sent his shadow on before, to prepare man for the real thing.

The Bible is not about religion. It tells you about the things that came before, but this information comes to you not so that you can make a religion out of it, but rather so that you can recognize God. The Bible is not about ceremonial observation of anything. More than anything else it is a revelation of reality. It is a revelation of the reality that is found in

Christ Jesus, that is, in the true God. In truth: God is. God is what he is, and he is who he is. God's name is I Am which means what I am saying now. God is Reality Personified. Apart from God there is nothing that is real. If God is standing before you, then that which is real is standing before you. The Bible is a revelation of reality.

The path to enlightenment may be found when you accept that you might not really know what is true. When you recognize that you might be lacking in correct understanding then you become teachable. If you are like me, and earnestly desire to know the truth about God, and about everything else in the world, then you must set aside everything that you think is right, and listen to God. A student must be teachable, and must respect the knowledge and understanding of the Teacher. If you don't respect your Teacher, and arrogantly hold to what you believe, then how can you possibly learn?

Proverbs 3:5
Trust in the Lord with all your heart and lean not on your own understanding; ... (NIV84)

This is how the Bible says what I just said. You must not rely on what you think is true. And then you must open yourself, as a little child does, with his or her mother and/or father, and listen to what God says, and trust in what he says, that is, in what the Bible says, and trust in him too. You must. This is how it works. It works no other way.

Mark 4:26–29
He also said, "This is what the kingdom of God is like. A man scatters seed on the ground. [27] Night and day, whether he sleeps or gets up, the seed sprouts and grows, though he does not know how. [28] All by itself the soil produces grain— first the stalk, then the head, then the full kernel in the head. 29 As soon as the grain is ripe, he puts the sickle to it, because the harvest has come." (NIV84)

Read this passage very carefully. Read it over and over until you see what it is saying. This is a critical passage regarding your walk in the light toward the Living God. Notice that the farmer (that's you) plants the seed (reads the Bible) into the ground (your spiritually receptive heart) and then the seed sprouts and grows even though you don't know how nor do you see it happen. God makes the seed sprout and grow within your heart and the seed itself has life within it, and that life blossoms within you to eternal life. The life comes from God as it does in the natural world too. This means that when you read it, it is not important that you

understand fully what you are reading, as the understanding takes time to sprout and grow, but when it does sprout and grow, then you have the harvest, that is, you do understand it.

Now, the farmer is a reasonable farmer, that is, he has faith in his seed. He plants the seed in the ground and then he doesn't dig it up again to see if it is growing. He believes in his seed. He plants it knowing that God will make it grow. The good farmer must do his part however. He must look after it and keep it in mind. Whoever heard of a farmer that plants his fields and then goes away and leaves them untended until harvest? That is not the way things work. He might not know how the seed grows, but he does know that he must keep the weeds away, and he knows that he must keep the bugs and animals out of the field as well as he can. What I am saying is that the farmer keeps his focus on his job, but he also trusts in God, for God to do his part.

> **Luke 10:21**
> **At that time Jesus, full of joy through the Holy Spirit, said, "I praise you, Father, Lord of heaven and earth, because you have hidden these things from the wise and learned, and revealed them to little children. Yes, Father, for this was your good pleasure. (NIV84)**

> **Matthew 18:3**
> **And he said: "I tell you the truth, unless you change and become like little children, you will *never* enter the kingdom of heaven. (NIV84)**

A person that wishes to learn from God must come to him like a little child comes to his or her mother or father (did you notice Jesus said this was mandatory). What this means is that you must trust in God, that is, trust that God will make the seeds of the Word of God grow within you; but you must plant them and let them grow, and you must trust that what your Father tells you is correct, that is, trust that the Bible is correct.

Suppose I like to tinker around in the garage on Saturday mornings, rebuilding my antique automobile. And suppose that I have a little daughter, or son, and I take her or him out into the garage each Saturday morning and explain all of the workings of the internal combustion engine, and the workings of each and every other system that makes up a working automobile. At first, when I describe the pistons, and the valves, and the rotating crankshaft, and camshaft, and the fuel system, and the electrical system and all the rest, my child will understand almost nothing of what I have been talking about. But, weekend after weekend, and after

disassembly and reassembly, and explanation after explanation, my child will soon understand everything that I understand about cars. My child believes in me and will therefore listen to me as I describe all of this, believing that I am speaking the truth. Because of my child's faith in me, and their obedient listening, they will learn. That is how learning works. That is how learning from God works too.

The so called wise and learned people of the world rely on their own understanding and reasoning ability. Worldly people want to succeed in the world and so they follow the world's acceptable path. They follow the path that elevates man's importance and deny the existence of God. They are prideful and puffed up about what they think. They think that what they think matters. They establish places of higher education that are dictated to everything that is not about God. They say that the universe is an accident and that we can master it. We can learn to control our own destiny. We can be our own masters. This is the same old story. This is Satan's story.

The wise and learned say, 'we know, or we will learn', but the humble and obedient say, 'teach me, Oh Lord.' You have to choose which authority you will listen to. The truth cannot be both ways. You must come to God and seek understanding just like a five-year-old child comes to his or her mother and asks why this is so or why that is so. When a child asks for understanding, that child expects to receive it; the child opens him or herself to the answer and accepts that the answer given is true. Eventually the child does get enough pieces of the puzzle to piece together the complete and satisfying answer.

I need to point out something here and that is that you don't abandon reason when you come to the Bible. The Bible is a very reasonable book. You must be reasonable and seek to understand what you are reading. I have heard many times the skeptic's proverb, Faith is believing in the unbelievable. This proverb is witty, yes, but it is a proverb of ignorance. Understanding is a reasonable thing and depends upon grasping the individual parts and seeing how they all fit together. Take for example the story of Moses leading the children of Israel out of Egypt and through the Red Sea. This story is completely reasonable, because we know that God, the Creator of Heaven and Earth, can do anything that he wants to do. God can reasonably part the sea, if he wants to, and it is reasonable for us to understand and accept this. In fact, it is not reasonable to believe that God can't do such a thing. The important thing in a story like Moses

and the Red Sea, is not what the Bible says happened, but rather why it happened in that way. You ask God to reveal to you why he chose to lead the people out of Egypt through the Red Sea, and what does that all mean? The stories in the Bible are very strange, granted, but it is because God is telling a story behind the story. True wisdom comes when you can understand that spiritual story.

What I mean is this: God, who can do anything (right?) could have snapped his fingers and presto, every single Egyptian dropped dead on the spot, and then the Israelites simply took over the country that was left. God could have orchestrated the events exactly that way, but he didn't because that would not have served his purpose. You should not presume to know God's purpose, unless the Lord has revealed to you. You should read the Bible and try to discern what God's purpose is. If you think that God is doing something that is not right, unfair, immoral, or whatever, then consider that you really don't know what is really going on or why. The Lord God is the very definition of what is right. Sometimes when reading the Bible Satan will try and stir up feelings of righteous indignation within you, but if he succeeds it is only because you don't know as much as you think you know.

You should be very careful about whom you listen to regarding the Bible and/or about the Lord God.

Mark 4:24
"Consider carefully what you hear," he continued. "With the measure you use, it will be measured to you—and even more. (NIV84)

You have only one Teacher and he is the Lord God. Listen to him and read the Bible.

When I am going about my life, I hear the Lord speak to me all the time. He speaks in my head in a voice that sounds just like my very own thoughts. He speaks to me in Bible. He is always showing me this or that with respect to what I have read in the Bible. As I watch movies, I hear his voice. As I read novels and such, I hear his voice. When people are talking to me and expressing themselves, I hear his voice. I did not notice any of this until I became a dedicated Bible reader.

I imagine that the Lord was speaking to me before I became a Bible reading believer, but I don't know. I know that he was drawing me toward himself, so I guess that he was communicating then, but I was so full of myself that I didn't really hear or know.

John 14:25–27
"All this I [Jesus] have spoken while still with you. ²⁶ But the Counselor, the Holy Spirit, whom the Father will send in my name, will teach you all things and will remind you of everything I have said to you. ²⁷ Peace I leave with you; my peace I give you. I do not give to you as the world gives. Do not let your hearts be troubled and do not be afraid. (NIV84)

Do you see? The Lord God Almighty, the Counselor, the Holy Spirit, whom the Father has sent, lives within you and will teach you all things. God is your Teacher. Listen to him. Read the Bible and let it work its magic on you. Let the words of the Bible sprout and grow within you until you receive the harvest. You must, however, read the Bible. The Bible is the storehouse of living seeds that can be planted within the willing and noble heart.

It is important to understand that the Counselor, the Holy Spirit, doesn't live inside of everyone. He only lives in the heart of those that have faith in God, that is, in Jesus Christ. A person must believe that Jesus is the One sent from God.

John 17:6–9
"I have revealed you to those whom you gave me out of the world. They were yours; you gave them to me and they have obeyed your word. ⁷ Now they know that everything you have given me comes from you. ⁸ For I gave them the words you gave me and they accepted them. They knew with certainty that I came from you, and they believed that you sent me. ⁹ I pray for them. I am not praying for the world, but for those you have given me, for they are yours.
(NIV84)

Looking back to the parable of the farmer and the seed, do you remember that both parties have a role to play? (I know that I am repeating myself here, but this is so very important.) God causes the Seed to grow, but you must prepare the soil and plant the seed. You have an active role to play in this. Without you, the seed will never do a thing within you. I can speak the Words of Life to people that have hardened their hearts (soil) and the seeds with not germinate and the seeds will not grow. You have an active role to play and I don't mean going to church and being a good Christian. I mean opening your heart to God and planting his seeds within you and actively working to keep your field free of weeds and undesirable forces, that is, being the sort of farmer that God likes.

2 Timothy 2:20–22
In a large house there are articles not only of gold and silver,
but also of wood and clay; some are for noble purposes and
some for ignoble. ²¹ *If a man cleanses himself* **from the lat-**
ter, he will be an instrument for noble purposes, made holy,
useful to the Master and prepared to do any good work.
²² Flee the evil desires of youth, and pursue righteousness,
faith, love and peace, along with those who call on the Lord
out of a pure heart. (NIV84)

Make sure that you see that the above passage says that you must cleanse yourself from ignoble things, and allow God to make you an instrument for noble purposes. This takes an active effort on your part. You must trust in God so that you will give up things that you are clinging to, so that God can transform you into his obedient child. Do you want to be loved by God? Is being loved by God something of value to you? Is there really anything else in the world that is worth more to you than your life? I don't mean physical life, I mean your eternal self with God.

The Revealed God

I DO NOT CALL MYSELF A teacher. I am not a teacher, at least about the things of God. I am a servant of God and I am very interested in pleasing my Master. It seems to me that what the Lord wants me to do is to write about these things, so that you can read them and under-stand. To please my God I must become your servant too. I must deny myself of things that distract me so that I can better serve you. Your understanding is important to God and is therefore important to me. So, I ask you not to think of me as being anything, but to keep your focus on God and your relationship with him. I am invisible. There is nothing that I have that God did not give to me. There is nothing that I understand that God did not put into my head, so to say. There is nothing in my head about God that did not come through the Bible. All I ever did is read the Bible and believe it was true. The way to God is through the Bible.

John 14:6
Jesus answered, "I am the way and the truth and the life.
No one comes to the Father except through me. (NIV84)

I said that the only way to God is through the Bible, and yet Jesus said that the only way to the Father was through him. What gives? Am I saying one thing, and then quoting another? Actually, I am not, because the Bible says that Jesus and the Bible are one and the same. Look at this.

John 1:1–5, 14
In the beginning was the Word, and the Word was with God, and the *Word was God*. [2] He was with God in the beginning. [3] Through him all things were made; without him nothing was made that has been made. [4] In him was life, and that life was the light of men. [5] The light shines in the darkness, but the darkness has not understood it. ...
[14] The Word became flesh and made his dwelling among us. We have seen his glory, the glory of the One and Only, who came from the Father, full of grace and truth. (NIV84)

In the beginning was the Word (Bible) and the Word was God.

Colossians 1:15
He [Jesus] is the image of the invisible God, the firstborn over all creation. (NIV84)

Jesus is the visible image of the invisible God, and so is the Bible. If you want to see God in the world today then you can look into the Bible.

You can look out into the world and see what God has made, and that will tell you much about him, but if you want to see him directly, then you must read the Bible. How else are you going to reliably see Jesus Christ? How, my friend? How?

There is a biblical principle that we should look at now. It is one of the principles that I call a Bible Axiom. This Bible Axiom is that you should not establish a doctrine without the testimony of two or three witnesses. What this means is that if you are going to say that Jesus was resurrected, then you need two or three Scriptures that say so—not just one. (The resurrection by the way is supported my many Scriptures, so it is very well established.) But I have said that Jesus is the Word of God, in human form, and I have used John chapter one to support this concept, but I need another Scripture before I can know that this is a true doctrine.

Revelation 19:11–16
I saw heaven standing open and there before me was a white horse, whose rider is called Faithful and True. With justice he judges and makes war. [12] His eyes are like blazing fire, and on his head are many crowns. He has a name written on him that no one knows but he himself. [13] He is dressed in a robe dipped in blood, *and his name is the Word of God*. [14] The armies of heaven were following him, riding on white horses and dressed in fine linen, white and clean. [15] Out of his mouth comes a sharp sword with which to strike down the nations. "He will rule them with an iron scepter." He treads the winepress of the fury of the wrath of God

Almighty. [16] On his robe and on his thigh he has this name written: king of kings and lord of lords. (NIV84)

Here we see Jesus leading the armies of heaven and coming to put an end to the Beast and his kingdom, and we see that this Jesus has the name Word of God, so we now see the second witness. Jesus Christ and the Holy Bible are both physical manifestations of the invisible God.

Deuteronomy 19:15
One witness is not enough to convict a man accused of any crime or offense he may have committed. A matter must be established by the testimony of two or three witnesses. (NIV84)

2 Corinthians 13:1
This will be my third visit to you. "Every matter must be established by the testimony of two or three witnesses." (NIV84)

The Axiom is itself supported by two witnesses. My point here, is a very important point. We want to stay right with God in our understanding of things. The way that we do that is to read the Bible and receive into ourselves what it says, but we must be careful that we stay with what God is saying. If a major point is being established in the Bible, then you will find more than one Scripture passage that supports that point, AND you will not find any Scripture passage that directly contradicts it.

When you come across a Scripture passage that seems to contradict some doctrine that you have thought to be right, you then must examine all of the Scriptures that relate, and allow the Lord God to reveal to you how they all fit together into the correct truth. This is how we grow. We know that every Scripture in the Bible is true, and we look for the one Truth that agrees with every Scripture.

1 Corinthians 4:6
Now, brothers, I have applied these things to myself and Apollos for your benefit, so that you may learn from us the meaning of the saying, "Do not go beyond what is written." Then you will not take pride in one man over against another. (NIV84)

This is a related Scripture. Paul advises us not to go beyond what is written. We must stay with the Bible and we must stay with the two witnesses axiom.

So, looking back at the Bible, and Jesus, we can see that they are one and the same. They are both physical revelations of God Almighty. This

is why the Bible is so important to us. If you want to really see God Almighty in the flesh, so to say, then look at his revealed form, which is Jesus Christ, and you can see Jesus Christ in the Bible.

Now, if someone or other were to come along and say that he has seen a revelation of Jesus Christ, and if that person were to say that Jesus spoke to him and told them things, well that is fine and dandy, but whatever Jesus was reported to have said must be examined in the light of all Scripture. This is how it works. Jesus is not going to come down from heaven and say things that contradict the Bible. If we didn't have the Bible then how could we possibly know, but we do have it, so we can read it and know it and then know if people are telling us true things or not.

> **Acts 17:11**
> **Now the Bereans were of more noble character than the Thessalonians, for they received the message with great eagerness and examined the Scriptures every day to see if what Paul said was true. (NIV84)**

Be like the Bereans. Read the Scriptures and judge everything by what they say. They are the standard by which everything else is measured.

Every Scripture to be Fulfilled

> **Matthew 5:17–20**
> **"Do not think that I have come to abolish the Law or the Prophets; I have not come to abolish them but to fulfill them. [18] I tell you the truth, until heaven and earth disappear, not the smallest letter, not the least stroke of a pen, will by any means disappear from the Law until everything is accomplished. [19] Anyone who breaks one of the least of these commandments and teaches others to do the same will be called least in the kingdom of heaven, but whoever practices and teaches these commands will be called great in the kingdom of heaven. [20] For I tell you that unless your righteousness surpasses that of the Pharisees and the teachers of the law, you will certainly not enter the kingdom of heaven. (NIV84)**

ERE WE SEE ANOTHER BIBLE Axiom. Jesus has not come to abolish the written Bible, but to fulfill it. As Jesus said here, every single statement in the Bible will happen just the way it says it will happen. To put this statement another way we can say that there are no spare-parts in the Bible, there are no contingency plans, no if this happens then that will happen, nothing like any of that. If the Bible says it,

then it will be just as the Bible says.

So, the Bible Axiom is this: Every single Scripture in the Bible will be fulfilled before the end. This is a very important thing to know. Please take the time to reread the above Scripture and then think on what it says, and think on what it means, and then reread again and think some more. The understanding of this passage unlocks many other things; it is what I call a Key Passage. It is a Key Passage because when we know that each and every verse will happen just as it says then we read them we read them knowing that they are alive; do you understand what I am saying? The Bible is alive; it's happening.

Some people think that Jesus came to do away with the Old Testament and establish a New Testament. In a way this is true, he did free us from the power of the Law, but he did not come to do away with the Old Testament Scriptures and establish a replacement volume of Scriptures. He makes this point very clear in the above passage.

> **2 Timothy 3:14–17**
> **But as for you, continue in what you have learned and have become convinced of, because you know those from whom you learned it, ¹⁵ and how from infancy you have known the holy Scriptures, which are able to make you wise for salvation through faith in Christ Jesus. ¹⁶ All Scripture is God-breathed and is useful for teaching, rebuking, correcting and training in righteousness, ¹⁷ so that the man of God may be thoroughly equipped for every good work. (NIV84)**

When Paul wrote those words, **"All Scripture is God breathed…"** which Scriptures do you imagine he was talking about? The New Testament was not in existence at that time, and the letters and other Christian works that were in circulation at that time were not considered Scripture. They were contemporary writings by contemporary people. If you read through the New Testament and pay attention to the quoted Scriptures you will see that virtually every point of Christianity was supported, that is, proved, by quoting Old Testament passages.

So please understand that everything written in the Old Testament will be fulfilled and nothing in it can be ignored, and nothing in it does not conform to everything revealed in the New Testament. It is all one coherent and consistent revelation of the same truth or reality.

However, the Old Testament Scriptures must be read with understanding and wisdom and be applied as God intended them to be. Things are not always so simple and things are frequently not what we think they

are. It is true that we are no longer under the Law of Moses, but which of the Ten Commandments can we break? You can break none of them. We, like Christ Jesus, are here to not abolish the Law, but to fulfill it. We are no longer under the authority of the Law, but we are the product of what the Law was intended to do.

> **Romans 2:14–15**
> **(Indeed, when Gentiles [if you are not a Jew then you are a Gentile], who do not have the law, do by nature things required by the law, they are a law for themselves, even though they do not have the law, 15 since they show that the requirements of the law are written on their hearts, their consciences also bearing witness, and their thoughts now accusing, now even defending them.) (NIV84)**

When the Jews rejected the Christ, the Gospel message then went to the non-Jews, that is, to the Gentiles. This passage is talking about Gentile believers that believe in Jesus Christ and have the life-giving Spirit within them, that is, they are born-again.

Speaking Bible

THE ONLY KIND OF SPIRITUAL information that I have any interest in learning is that which comes to us from God. Spiritual information that comes from any other source ultimately comes from Satan— really. There are real spiritual forces at work in the world that have no allegiance to God, and to follow their direction will certainly lead you to eternal death. Every spirit that is not in Christ is destined for destruction—100%. That is the reality. As the saying goes, read the end of the book. Each and every spiritual being is either in God or not, and there is only one authorized source of spiritual information and that source is the Bible—period; end of story; sorry but it is true. (Actually I am not sorry, but supremely thankful.)

As I have said before, the Bible and Jesus are in a very real way, one and the same. To really know the Bible is to really know Jesus Christ. A person that doesn't know the Bible may know of Jesus Christ, and that person, because of the testimony of other believers may believe in Jesus Christ, but that person doesn't actually know Jesus Christ. Such knowledge comes to one through the Bible. One can know Jesus Christ by direct revelation, but all such revelation will agree with the Bible and unless it does agree with the Bible, then it cannot be relied on.

> **John 17:6–8**
> **"I have revealed you to those whom you gave me out of**

the world. They were yours; you gave them to me and they have obeyed your word. ⁷ Now they know that everything you have given me comes from you. ⁸ For I gave them the words you gave me and they accepted them. They knew with certainty that I came from you, and they believed that you sent me. (NIV84)

Please reread the above verse and think of the Jesus/Bible connection. The Bible has revealed God to those in the world that belong to God. We believers know that every word of the Bible ultimately comes from God. Jesus gave us the words of revelation through the Bible and we have accepted the Bible's words as beings God's words. We know with certainty that the Bible came from God and that God gave to us the Bible. Do you see how that works? My friend, if you reject the Bible, you are rejecting Jesus Christ.

Now, I have been reading the Bible for many years and despite the fact that I don't have much of it actually memorized I do know what it says. The knowledge that I have is more along the line of knowing what it means than knowing the exact wording. This is okay, because I only know a translation anyway and no translation is going to be exact in its wording. This too is okay because it is not the words that mean anything, but the meaning. This is why translations are just as good as the original. Do you understand what I am saying? There are many people in the world that know exactly what the original languages say in the Scriptures that do not know what the Scriptures really mean. Revelation from God comes in the form of understanding and not in exact wording.

When I walk about in the world I hear God's gentle whisper talking to me, explaining to me what this means and what that means and so on and so on. His gentle whisper talks to me in Bible. What I mean by that is that when I am seeing something or watching someone I see the connections between what I have read in the Bible and what I am seeing and hearing. What I am saying to you now is very subtle. Very little things come to me this way. I see this; I see that; I hear this and I hear that; little things; subtle things.

Let me try and give you a little example. Say when someone at work says something very nice to me, I hear the words and also I hear many other things that the Bible says about me and other people. I hear the verbal words of praise, but I also know that the only praise that matters is that which comes from God. God may, or may not, tell me why the person just said what they said, and if he does it will be in Bible too;

God might point out to me this or that about the speaker and anyway, it is pretty impossible for me to explain this to you, because each case is so unique and the revelation so subtle.

When I watch something on the television or read in a book, God usually says something to me about that too, always in Bible. When I read of some historical event God is there explaining to me what he was doing and why as it relates to the Bible scenario as it is revealed in the Bible.

Now, my point in telling you all of this is that the stories in the Bible are not just historical events. In fact, that is really a very minor part of them. The Bible is alive. What it says to us is alive. Everything that it reveals to us is for us today. I don't mean rules and lists of good things and bad things, but of motivations, and causes and effects and much much more. Through the Bible, God is revealed to us, and through our relationship with the Bible, we grow more like God in just the same way that your son or daughter might grow more like you as they do things with you. The Bible is alive and we must live with it. The Bible must be alive in our hearts. Who cares if you have the whole thing memorized; unless it is alive within you it profits you nothing.

For the Bible to be alive in you, you must believe in it—really believe in it.

One of the assumptions that I make when writing about the Bible is that you know your Bible. I must make this assumption. I can't talk about the Bible in any meaningful way unless you yourself know what has happened in the Bible. If I talk about Abraham, then you must know the stories about him, who he is, and what he did and such. The Bible must become our language. I talk to you in Bible events and point out meanings and things to you within the context of the Bible events. The Bible is our spiritual language. If you don't speak Bible then how are you going to understand what I am saying? If you don't understand Bible then you must go back and read your Bible. Read it every day. I don't mean that you have to understand all of it. You just need to know the language. The language I speak is Bible and the language God speaks to us with is also Bible. In your eagerness to know, you must not bypass this step. It would be like teaching children to spell before you teach them the letters. We must all speak the same language.

Now, my friend, how do you know if I am speaking the truth to you? How can you know? The only reliable way is for you to know your Bible and listen to what I am writing while letting God speak to you in Bible.

At first you need to read much more Bible than anything else. After you can speak Bible pretty well, then you can see what other people have to say about God.

There is a big religious group in the world that calls themselves a Church and they really promote family values and clean living, but they also deny that the Bible is the Word of God. The more you listen to them the more you realize that they don't really know the Lord Jesus Christ at all. There are red flags popping up everywhere whenever I hear their doctrine. These red flags, these direct contradictions to the Bible, tell me that they are not speaking God's words and that I should stay far away from them. God does not say one thing yesterday and another today and yet another tomorrow.

> **Hebrews 13:8**
> **Jesus Christ is the same yesterday and today and forever.**
> **(NIV84)**

If you want to know Jesus Christ, then know your Bible. I imagine that learning to speak fluent Bible takes about as long as learning to speak fluently in any other language. It takes time. It takes some people more time and others less time, but we all need to learn nonetheless. And you don't have to be fluent in a language to be better off than not knowing anything. Becoming fluent in Bible is something that takes a lifetime. Even an infant is a full member of the family.

The Voice of Christ

> **John 10:24–27**
> **The Jews gathered around him, saying, "How long will you keep us in suspense? If you are the Christ, tell us plainly." [25] Jesus answered, "I did tell you, but you do not believe. The miracles I do in my Father's name speak for me, [26] but you do not believe because you are not my sheep. [27] My sheep listen to my voice; I know them, and they follow me. (NIV84)**

HEN ONE HAS A RELATIONSHIP with the Lord, you just know when he is speaking, but understand that whatever he says to you will not contradict Scripture; this is a sort of double check. In an extreme example we have all heard of crazy people saying that they heard the voice of God tell them to do some clearly evil thing, but God does not contradict himself. What he tells us today will agree with every verse in the Bible. God does not tell people to kill other people and such.

This is a very subtle thing here. People are killed in the Bible but God will not ask you to do the killing. If someone desperately needs killing then God will do the deed if in fact the deed need be done. God is just and will do what is right and he will carry out just judgment. We, on the other hand, cannot be trusted to act as judge. Even King David, of whom God said that he was a man after his own heart, was not allowed to build the Temple of the Lord because he had shed blood in battle.

The way things work is that if some person must die to fulfill prophecy, it is not for you, my dear brother or sister, to do the deed. Someone else will do the killing or whatever. You are called to be like Jesus Christ himself. Jesus never took matters into his own hands. If God's plan calls for some person or other to die then he or she will die, but let it not be by our hand.

There are many very subtle situations where God will guide a person along the course of biblical truth. It is very important that you know your Bible well and that you listen to the voice of the Spirit within you as he guides you through life. Again, if you do not know your Bible then it is very difficult to know the word of the Lord and to actually follow him. Jesus said above that his sheep know his voice; what voice is that? Do you imagine that his voice is different than the revealed Holy Scriptures? God's voice is quiet and subtle and will lead you into all holiness and gentleness and peace. Even if God's voice leads you into your physical death then your physical death is the best thing for you. If God loves you then everything that he does on your behalf is for your benefit.

Romans 8:28
And we know that in all things God works for the good of those who love him, who have been called according to his purpose. (NIV84)

Now, when the all-knowing and all-powerful God Almighty tells you something in your heart of hearts, how much authority does his guidance carry? Is there any authority that is greater, any at all? When God is speaking to you in Bible then the words that you 'hear' carry complete authority.

God Has the Power to Fulfill His Word

Isaiah 46:8–11
"Remember this, fix it in mind, take it to heart, you rebels. [9]
Remember the former things, those of long ago; I am God,

and there is no other; I am God, and there is none like me.
[10] I make known the end from the beginning, from ancient
times, what is still to come. I say: My purpose will stand,
and I will do all that I please. [11] From the east I summon a
bird of prey; from a far-off land, a man to fulfill my pur-
pose. What I have said, that will I bring about; what I have
planned, that will I do. (NIV84)

G*OD'S WORD, THE BIBLE, CANNOT* fail, and neither will any aspect of the Plan of God fail to be fulfilled at its appointed time.

Matthew 24:35
Heaven and earth will pass away, but my words will never
pass away. (NIV84)

Mark 13:31
Heaven and earth will pass away, but my words will never
pass away. (NIV84)

Luke 21:33
Heaven and earth will pass away, but my words will never
pass away. (NIV84)

The Lord God Almighty spoke these words through his Son Jesus Christ and they are recorded exactly the same in three Gospels. That makes them very important words. (Any time you see anything repeated in the Bible, take special notice of it.) The Bible has all authority. Look at this passage…

Matthew 28:18
Then Jesus came to them and said, "All authority in heav-
en and on earth has been given to me. (NIV84)

Remember that Jesus and the Bible are one and the same. All authority has been given to Jesus and that means that not one word of the Bible will ever fail.

There are many things in the Bible's prophecies and each and every one of them will be fulfilled exactly as the Bible says that will. None of them are optional. None of them are conditional. The world is going down the exact path that God says that it will go down. Nothing anyone can do can change even the smallest thing.

I hate war as much as anyone else does, but that doesn't mean that I would ever protest any war and lobby my leaders to stop the war. Such things are not my responsibility. What is written will come to pass.

Matthew 24:6
You will hear of wars and rumors of wars, but see to it that

you are not alarmed. Such things must happen, but the end is still to come. (NIV84)

My job, as it were, is to obey the Lord and grow in my likeness to him and in my understanding of him. The world will go the way the world goes.

The Bible tells us to obey our government and to honor those in power. That is what I shall do. If people in government do wrong then God will deal with them. It is not for me to judge.

Romans 13:1–7
Everyone must submit himself to the governing authorities, for there is no authority except that which God has established. The authorities that exist have been established by God. [2] Consequently, he who rebels against the authority is rebelling against what God has instituted, and those who do so will bring judgment on themselves. [3] For rulers hold no terror for those who do right, but for those who do wrong. Do you want to be free from fear of the one in authority? Then do what is right and he will commend you. [4] For he is God's servant to do you good. But if you do wrong, be afraid, for he does not bear the sword for nothing. He is God's servant, an agent of wrath to bring punishment on the wrongdoer. [5] Therefore, it is necessary to submit to the authorities, not only because of possible punishment but also because of conscience.
[6] This is also why you pay taxes, for the authorities are God's servants, who give their full time to governing. [7] Give everyone what you owe him: If you owe taxes, pay taxes; if revenue, then revenue; if respect, then respect; if honor, then honor. (NIV84)

The important thing for you to understand in this, is that God has told you personally, what you are to do, and that is what you should do. It is not your responsibility to fix the world or make the world a better place. You cannot fix the world. The world is going the way that it is going and there is nothing that you can do about that. Your duty is to God and to your fellow man, one-on-one.

There is such a thing as destiny. The world is destined to the end that is foretold, but your destiny is not foretold. You have choices to make. You can either obey God or not. You can do the things that God tells you to do, or you can put your faith in the world, and try to save it, but you cannot do both. The world has been judged and all those people that have their faith in the world will go down when the world goes down. If

you have faith in God, then you will be saved from the fate of the world. This is a test of your faith. Do you have faith in God? Is your faith in the things of the world?

Clear Warnings and Proof of God

GOD HAS WARNED US, THROUGH the Bible, what happens to people that remain in rebellion towards God. All mankind has some understanding of what constitutes wrongful behavior and what sort of life God desires for us to live. We all know. Everyone around the world knows on some level just what wrong doing will result in. Pretty much everyone has heard of the Noah's flood and the reason for it. The Bible is a verbal warning to us all. It is a message from God warning us against rebellion and wooing us to God.

The Bible gives us a historical perspective concerning cause and effect with respect to God. By reading them we can see what happened in the past because of obedience and disobedience, and the Bible also tells us what is going to happen in the future because of sin and rebellion and because of faithfulness and obedience.

The prophecy Scriptures also serve as an identification for God. God foretells events sometimes thousands of years before they are fulfilled and no one else can do that. God reveals to man through the Bible things that happened long ago and things that will happen long into the future and his prophecies are exactly correct. There is a common misconception that the prophecies are vague and can be fulfilled by any number of events, but this is not correct. They are exact and when they are fulfilled the fulfillment is clear and obvious. Did you know that 483 years before the event of Jesus' Triumphal Entry into Jerusalem, that was foretold in unmistakable detail? Yes, this is true. We will look into that later in the book. Psalm 22 describes the crucifixion of Jesus approximately 1000 years before the event. There are many such examples in Scripture.

Isaiah 44:6–8
"This is what the Lord says— Israel's King and Redeemer, the Lord Almighty: I am the first and I am the last; apart from me there is no God. ⁷ Who then is like me? Let him proclaim it. Let him declare and lay out before me what has happened since I established my ancient people, and what is yet to come— yes, let him foretell what will come. ⁸ Do not tremble, do not be afraid. Did I not proclaim this and foretell it long ago? You are my witnesses. Is there any God

besides me? No, there is no other Rock; I know not one."
(NIV84)

Isaiah 42:8–9
"I am the Lord; that is my name! I will not give my glory to
another or my praise to idols. ⁹ See, the former things have
taken place, and new things I declare; before they spring
into being I announce them to you." (NIV84)

Isaiah 48:5–6
Therefore I told you these things long ago; before they happened I announced them to you so that you could not say,
'My idols did them; my wooden image and metal god ordained them.' ⁶ You have heard these things; look at them
all. Will you not admit them? "From now on I will tell you
of new things, of hidden things unknown to you. (NIV84)

One of the major purposes of this book is to show what the Bible says
is going to happen in the world soon. The Bible foretold, many thousands
of years ago, exactly what was going to happen in the world today. We are
lining up for the big finale. These prophecies serve to prove the Bible's
accuracy and God's power and they also serve to guide us away from the
path of destruction and into the path of life with God.

One of the most interesting things about the way the Bible is written is
that it tells the story of man from the very beginning to the very end, so
that even though we live only during the time that we live we can benefit
from seeing the entire picture. We don't have to see the destruction that
comes during the time of the Beast to understand what it is about and how
we can escape a similar fate. There is a saying today about it being easy
to be a Monday morning quarterback and that is true. It means that after
the game is played it is easy to say what the team should have done to
win and what the team should not have done. It is much easier after the
fact to make such comments. Well the Bible is written so that you are a
Monday morning quarterback. You can see the whole game played from
beginning to end and then return back to your present time and make
better decisions than you otherwise would have. Do you understand what
I am saying? We see the whole world going up in smoke and we also
see how to personally escape the world's fate. With this knowledge we
can choose the better path. If we are wise we can choose a better path.

Path for Our Feet

THIS BRINGS US TO ANOTHER major purpose of the Bible, and that is the role of Teacher and Guide. I hear people all the time saying to me that they think that they are going to heaven because they are 'good people.' Is that the way it works? Do you know this? How do you know this? Without the Bible such speculation could really be the only way to think, but since we have the Bible, we should read it, and listen to it, and learn from it, so that we can know what it takes to get into heaven; to know what it takes to escape spiritual death, and enter into a living relationship with the Creator of heaven and earth. We need the Bible for this. We cannot rely on our own thinking. Remember earlier we saw that the Bible warns us against leaning on your own understanding. We must not think that what we think matters; God tells us what is—this is as it should be, as it must be, as it is.

> **Psalm 119:105**
> **Your word is a lamp to my feet and a light for my path.**
> **(NIV84)**

> **Deuteronomy 17:18–20**
> **When he [Israel's king] takes the throne of his kingdom, he is to write for himself on a scroll a copy of this law, taken from that of the priests, who are Levites. [19] It is to be with him, and he is to *read it all the days of his life* so that he may learn to revere the Lord his God and follow carefully all the words of this law and these decrees [20] and not consider himself better than his brothers and turn from the law to the right or to the left. Then he and his descendants will reign a long time over his kingdom in Israel.** (NIV84)

Without the Bible, we cannot know what we must do. Without the light of the Bible, we are in darkness. When we are in darkness, we cannot see the truth. We just can't.

Our very life is intimately tied to the Bible, your life and my life. If I develop the power of my mind so that I can explode rocks, but do not have an intimate relationship with God then I am nothing. If I can recall in exact recollection every word of 10,000 books, but do not have God then again I am nothing. Only God and his heaven will remain. This is true whether or not you know it or believe it. This is what the Bible says and God gave you the Bible so that you too can know this.

If you chose to ignore the Bible then you are a dry leaf blown by the winds of fate. If you chose to bond with the Lord God then you are anchored to the immovable rock and the winds will blow over you or

around you, but will not be able to move you.

Every Word Will Be Fulfilled

I HAVE SAID THIS BEFORE, BUT feel it is just too important not to repeat again, and that is, that every single word in the Bible will come to pass. This is so important to understand. Every single word of the Bible will come to pass.

> **Isaiah 55:8–11**
> **"For my thoughts are not your thoughts, neither are your ways my ways," declares the Lord. ⁹ "As the heavens are higher than the earth, so are my ways higher than your ways and my thoughts than your thoughts. ¹⁰ As the rain and the snow come down from heaven, and do not return to it without watering the earth and making it bud and flourish, so that it yields seed for the sower and bread for the eater, ¹¹ *so is my word that goes out from my mouth: It will not return to me empty, but will accomplish what I desire and achieve the purpose for which I sent it.* (NIV84)**

Isaiah is telling us, or rather the Spirit of the Lord God Almighty is telling us, that God's thoughts are not our thoughts, so therefore we must be instructed. We totally need a Teacher to show us God's thoughts, and to show us his ways. We see from this passage that God speaks his words, first, and then the words will have the power to germinate and grow into compete fulfillment. God speaks these words beforehand because he loves us and wants us to understand and he wants us to take heed so that the terrible things that are coming will not destroy us along with the world. We are dearly loved children that earnestly desire to know the will of our Father, and we listen to him and learn, so that we too will not be swept away with all those that do not know the truth.

If you think about this, you can ask yourself what the purpose is of publishing what is going to happen, if it's not to give us warning in time to do something about it. I mean, if God is all powerful (and he is), and he has determined what exactly is going to happen (and it will therefore happen), then what would be the point of telling anyone if not to give us warning? This warning is given to us in love so that we may respond and not be lost, so my friend, listen to the warnings and benefit.

> **Isaiah 46:11**
> **From the east I summon a bird of prey; from a far-off land,**

a man to fulfill my purpose. What I have said, that will I bring about; what I have planned, that will I do. (NIV84)

Jeremiah 1:12
The Lord said to me, "You have seen correctly, for I am watching to see that my word is fulfilled." (NIV84)

Ezekiel 12:21–25
The word of the Lord came to me: ²² "Son of man, what is this proverb you have in the land of Israel: 'The days go by and every vision comes to nothing'? ²³ Say to them, 'This is what the Sovereign Lord says: I am going to put an end to this proverb, and they will no longer quote it in Israel.' Say to them, 'The days are near when every vision will be fulfilled. ²⁴ For there will be no more false visions or flattering divinations among the people of Israel. ²⁵ But I the Lord will speak what I will, and it shall be fulfilled without delay. For in your days, you rebellious house, I will fulfill whatever I say, declares the Sovereign Lord.' " (NIV84)

People have been hiding from the fear of biblical prophecy since the beginning of biblical prophecy. People have been saying that it won't happen, but God assures us that it shall.

The fact that every word in the Bible will be fulfilled is very helpful to us in understanding the Bible. We know that every verse is going to happen, and so when we are trying to understand the scenario that will play out, we must account for every verse.

When Jesus came and walked the earth many of the Jews totally believed in the coming of the Christ, but they were expecting the coming of the reigning King. They thought this because the Bible talks about him in this way, however the Bible also talks about him coming and being rejected and then being killed. And the Bible talks about him being before David and also being a priest forever along the lines of Melchizedek. All of these passages must be fulfilled. He must come, he must be killed for our sins, and he must reign forever. The Pharisees of old were guilty of what I see every day, and that is, believing in the Scriptures that they wanted to believe in, and ignoring the others. This is a very dangerous thing to do.

When we come to God like little children, and listen to him in the Word, then we hear every verse and we ask the Lord, 'How can this be?' We do not ignore anything, no matter how inconvenient it may be. Every single word in the Bible will be fulfilled, and we must place them into the biblical scenario, if we want to see everything that is going to happen.

Examples: Jesus

B ELOW ARE SOME EXAMPLES OF prophecies and their fulfillment.

> **Isaiah 7:14 - Matthew 1:22-23**
> **Hosea 11:1 – Matthew 2:14-15**
> **Jeremiah 31:15 – Matthew 2:16-18**
> **Zechariah 11:12-13 – Matthew 26:14-16**
> **Matthew 26:53-56**

This last one is very interesting to me. Jesus knew what the Scriptures said and they predicted a very grim scenario for him, and yet, even though he had the power to stop what was written he still allowed every Bible verse concerning him to play out. Jesus did this because he was completely and totally obedient to the Father, and he knew that what the Father wanted was the right thing. It is one thing to be martyred for your beliefs, it is all together a different thing to willingly and obediently offer yourself as a sacrifice for others when you have the immediate ability to put a stop to it. Do you have that much faith in God? Please think deeply about this. Do you really have faith to suffer like that, for Christ, when you could stop it if you wanted to? This is just something to think about.

There are many verses that talk about you in the Bible. They inform you about certain things that are likely to happen to you, and about certain things that you will want to do but must not do. Are you going to remain obedient, and do what the Bible tells you to do? If you wish the passages that speak of the believers to be true for you, that is, if you wish to remain a believer, then you will remain obedient to God, and what is written, just like Jesus did.

Do Not Go Beyond What is Written

T HIS IS ANOTHER AXIOM THAT I have previously mentioned and that is that we should be careful of going beyond what the Scriptures say. What this means is that we don't hold beliefs on topics that the Bible doesn't have anything to say about, such as where God came from. There are many topics that fall into this category: cigarette smoking, extreme sports, caffeine intake and whatever else that the Bible doesn't talk about. If you feel that any or all of the above are wrong then don't do them, but don't worry about what others believe

on disputable topics.

If God hasn't revealed something in the Bible, then we just don't need to know it, and we should very quickly accept that. We must remain obedient and that means listening to the Father and receiving from him what he says.

Zeal is a fine thing, but we must take care that our zeal is in accordance with the truth.

> **Proverbs 19:2**
> **It is not good to have zeal without knowledge, nor to be hasty and miss the way.** (NIV84)
>
> **Romans 10:2**
> **For I can testify about them that they are zealous for God, but their zeal is not based on knowledge.** (NIV84)
>
> **Romans 12:11**
> **Never be lacking in zeal, but keep your spiritual fervor, serving the Lord.** (NIV84)

We see in these passages that zeal is a good thing, but it must be a zeal that is in accordance with the truth. I see people all of the time being zealous in wrong ways. They are hopping up and down Bible thumpers, but they have missed the boat when it comes to really knowing the Lord. They are frequently so filled with righteous indignation that they condemn others in their efforts to justify themselves. Remember my friends, we are but little children. We seek the Lord of truth in all love and sincerity.

> **1 Timothy 1:5**
> **The goal of this command is love, which comes from a pure heart and a good conscience and a sincere faith.** (NIV84)

I find this passage to be wonderful in my sight. It tells us the goal, the goal that we should be aiming for. If love is truly your goal, then your zeal will be in the right place.

Section Summary: The Purpose of the Bible

LET US BRIEFLY GO OVER the purpose of the Bible again. The Bible is God revealed to us. The Bible is also to reveal to us the truth about everything spiritual. Every other source of information concerning spiritual matters is suspect; more than suspect, it is almost guaranteed to be wrong. God gave us his testimony concerning the true source of the Bible's information through many signs, miracles and wonders. We have many eye witness accounts of these supernatu-

ral events so that we can know exactly what happened, and that these events came from God. Each of us also has an inner testimony that urges us to seek and obey God.

One of the things that I have discovered in my study of the Bible prophecies is that they are completely and totally remarkable in their subtlety, and in how they all fit together so perfectly. For me this was quite a revelation. I found that the more I saw their perfection, the more faith I had in everything else in the Bible. It is my hope, and my aim, that I can show you the beauty of this, as this book progresses.

The Bible is the only reliable source of information concerning all spiritual matters. We must know these things if we are going to avoid sin and become holy. Without the Bible we would be stumbling around in the darkness, but for us the Bible is light that shines down on the truth. The Bible is truly wonderful.

The Bible is also the only reliable source of information regarding what is going on in the world, and why things are the way they are, and where things are going. Through the Bible we can know these things and without the Bible we can know nothing.

I would like to point out something else about the Bible that I haven't yet mentioned and that is that it shall be an eternal record for all of God's angels and children, which will endure forever and ever, concerning what the effect of sin is. Sin is BAD, and the Bible is a chronicle of just how bad, and why it is bad, and of just what sin is. This is big stuff.

The Real Story
Chapter Two

✿

MUCH OF THE INFORMATION IN the Bible is hidden within its symbolic language. It is important to understand this language. This hidden information isn't hidden in any real code, but rather the most important aspects of the Bible's stories are to be found in the meaning of the stories and not in the stories themselves. Certain words and/or phrases have a deeper meaning, that is, a spiritual meaning, than just the literal understanding. In this section I will be talking about some of the more important images in the Bible and what they mean in terms of the Big Picture.

Truth and Reality

WHAT *TRUTH IS, IS SIMPLE* enough; it is the opposite of a lie, however in the Bible, Truth means something a little different than that. Imagine that you have entered into some sort of Virtual Reality Pod, and within it, you can experience, just like it is completely real, an artificial reality. What I mean is, suppose that within the Pod, for example, you can fly like a bird. Imagine that within the Virtual Reality Pod it is so real, that you just can't tell the difference between what you experience within the pod, and real life. Imagine that this virtual reality pod is a whole body interface between your existing senses and some super computer that is capable of allowing you to see and smell and feel realistically all of the senses just like it was real. I am asking you to imagine something that you might see in a science fic-

tion movie. Can you imagine this, flying just like a bird, and not being able to sense the difference between real life and the virtual reality pod experience? (I am talking about some make-believe system like those in the films The Matrix or Avatar.) Imagine, though, that these make-believe virtual reality pods were actually real.

Now that you have imagined these make-believe virtual reality pods I want you to consider that our bodies are sort of like that. The real us, the spirit us, the us that was created in the image and likeness of God, does actually live inside a sort of virtual reality interface unit called a human body. Consider what I am saying and keep imagining. I know that this is going to sound a little strange and unfamiliar to your ears, but there is a truth in what I am saying. Because we are actually eternal spirit beings that live only temporarily in our human bodies we can think of our bodies and the whole physical universe as not being as real as we thought that they were.

We enter into the physical universe in a virtual-reality-suit that we call a human body, and we experience things as though they are completely real, but much of what we experience with these animal bodies is not actually real in the truest sense of the word. We humans are not like any of the other animals on this earth. We are actually spiritual beings, just like God and the angels, and we live within these animal bodies, these temporary reality interfaces, in a pseudo heaven that we call God's creation. God created an artificial reality within the real reality, that is, the physical universe is within heaven. Now I have said that we are in these temporary reality interfaces that we call our bodies, and I mean just that. God has made all of this, so as to be exceedingly real, but it is not as real as heaven is. I mean, our life in the physical world reality seems real enough, but the actual reality is heaven, or I should say that heaven is The Reality. This whole creation, the entire universe of physical energy and matter, is temporary and will be removed by God after it has served its purpose. That is not imaginary. That is the fact of the matter. The physical universe is temporary.

We, as actual spirit beings, are eternal, that is, we exist outside of time, but we are put into mortal bodies to live out a 'life span.' The experience is totally real, but the reality of it all is not actually real. This body we now live in will grow old and die, but we do not grow old, and cannot die in the same sense as the body dies.

The entire physical universe is actually nothing more than a huge virtual reality machine. Nothing in it is actually and truly real.

The Bible warns us not to fall in love with the artificial reality, that is, what the Bible calls the World, but rather to love God and his reality. I am fully aware that the universe is real and that our human bodies are real too, but I am also perfectly aware that we are really spirit being, created in the image and likeness of God, and that we are currently experiencing the physical universe in our temporary human bodies.

I know that this is a lot to grasp, but it is very important that you understand what I am trying to say. You, the real you, is a spirit person, and we call that person a soul, and your soul is now living within a temporary human body. You don't have to stay in that body forever, because that body will not last forever, but your soul nonetheless will exist for ever. After you have spent your time in the temporary universe you will then leave it and find yourself in the permanent universe which we call heaven. What I am telling you now is totally real and true. I am not using figures of speech or speaking in a parable. I am using modern words and modern ideas taken from science fiction stores to explain, but what I am saying is just what he Bible says about this universe.

1 John 2:15
Do not love the world or anything in the world. If anyone loves the world, the love of the Father is not in him. (NIV84)

John 12:25
The man who loves his life will lose it, while the man who hates his life in this world will keep it for eternal life. (NIV84)

My friend, you have to look deeply and carefully at those two passages and think on what they mean. I know that I am using non-traditional arguments in describing the Bible to you, but these ways of describing things are actually very close to reality. We are not to love the world more than God because the world is not really real. It is just some place where you can experience sin and still live. In heaven there can be no sin. In heaven it is impossible to truly understand sin. Here we can live with sin and grow to hate it or grow to love it. Here we can experience godlessness and also God. Here is the place of choosing.

Hebrews 12:26–29
At that time his voice shook the earth, but now he has promised, "Once more I will shake not only the earth but also the heavens." 27 The words "once more" indicate the removing of what can be shaken—that is, created things—so that what cannot be shaken may remain. 28 Therefore, since we are receiving a kingdom that cannot be shaken, let us be thankful,

and so worship God acceptably with reverence and awe, 29 for our "God is a consuming fire." (NIV84)

This passage is very bold. Everything that can be shaken, and we are told that this means everything that was created, (the whole physical universe), will be removed and the only thing that will remain is the eternal, that is, heaven, hell and the spiritual beings within. This passage also tells us that because the universe is only temporary we should keep our focus on God because God is a consuming fire, that is, God will remove the physical universe like wood is burned in a fire and is gone.

Unless you understand this temporary nature of the physical universe and of your natural life you will not be able to properly understand the Bible. As long as you think that the natural matters, then you will not focus your attention on what actually matters.

Hebrews 11:8–10
By faith Abraham, when called to go to a place he would later receive as his inheritance, obeyed and went, even though he did not know where he was going. 9 By faith he made his home in the promised land like a stranger in a foreign country; he lived in tents, as did Isaac and Jacob, who were heirs with him of the same promise. 10 For he was looking forward to the city with foundations, whose architect and builder is God. (NIV84)

Apart from Jesus, Abraham is the most important man that ever lived on the earth. We see here that he did not live for anything in this world. He lived for God and for heaven. This is very important. If you are a Christian then you are a partaker of the covenant that God made to Abraham. If you claim to be a partaker of his covenant then you must be like him. All that I have been saying about the physical universe being like an artificial virtual reality machine is just another way of saying what this is saying about Abraham. Abraham lived in the world, but he didn't put his faith in it, that is, he didn't believe it was more real than God and his heaven. Abraham lived in the world but lived for God.

Galatians 3:9
So those who have faith are blessed along with Abraham, the man of faith. (NIV84)

Abraham lived in the world as a stranger and he looked forward to the real existence, that is, he was waiting for the city that God made, that is, heaven. This is what I am talking about.

Hebrews 11:13–16
All these people were still living by faith when they died.
They did not receive the things promised; they only saw
them and welcomed them from a distance. And they admit-
ted that they were aliens and strangers on earth. ¹⁴ People
who say such things show that they are looking for a coun-
try of their own. ¹⁵ If they had been thinking of the country
they had left, they would have had opportunity to return.
¹⁶ Instead, they were longing for a better country—a heav-
enly one. Therefore God is not ashamed to be called their
God, for he has prepared a city for them. (NIV84)

So, when we consider the truth of all of this, the fact that the world does not matter and that heaven does matter, then we can begin to understand our true role or objective in life. It doesn't matter if you are considered successful in this world. It doesn't matter if you are comfortable here, or healthy here, or beautiful here, or wealthy here. What matters is that you have a living relationship here, with the living God who lives there, so that you have a home waiting for you when you depart this world, and that home is in heaven. Heaven is what is real. The physical universe is just a temporary place. Heaven is eternal and so are you my brothers and sisters.

Please remember that I am not talking about religion here. I am not talking about church. I am talking about God and living for him and his reality of Divine Love. Here we live in a reality dominated by selfishness. Here the mantra is me, me, me. In heaven it is love, love, love. Here it is about you and what you want; there it is about what love would have you do. Here, life is about money, power, sex, influence; there about harmony, peace, kindness, gentleness self-sacrifice. Here in your temporary human body you must choose which reality is more important.

Light & Darkness

I HAVE BEEN TALKING ABOUT THE real reality. If you are truly read-ing and listening to the Bible, then the Bible will shed light on what is real, and that is why the truth of the Bible is called light. This light shines on what is real, or makes it visible to you. Without the Bible you cannot see what is real, and so you find that you are in darkness with respect to the truth. Without the Bible's light, money, power, sex and worldly comforts are all that you really see, but when you see past the world you can see into heaven and the real reality that is God. The Bible allows you to see the effects of sin and the total destruction that

it causes, and you can also see the fruit of the Spirit of God and the eternity that it sustains. Your ability to see comes to you because of the Bible's revelations—light.

John 12:35–36
Then Jesus told them, "You are going to have the light just a little while longer. Walk while you have the light, before darkness overtakes you. The man who walks in the dark does not know where he is going. [36] Put your trust in the light while you have it, so that you may become sons of light." (NIV84)

Jesus was talking about himself here. He was/is the Light and that means that he was/is the Truth. The Truth is what is real and lasting, that is, God and his real universe-heaven.

Jesus revealed to us the reality of the Lord God Almighty and the real reality of heaven. When Jesus says that he is the Light this means that his life, his walk, his attitudes and everything about him was exactly the way that we should live. His very life bore witness to the Truth. His very life was a perfect example of how we should live. He is not an extreme example, he is the perfect example. That is what being the light means. Jesus lived for the eternal life and not the physical life. Much of what Jesus did and said seems strange to us because we are accustomed to the world and take our meaning from the world. But, Jesus spoke and acted as one who came from heaven and only lived for heaven and only considered heaven, that is, God.

Jesus lived for heaven because he knew that only heaven matters. This world is passing away and everyone that loves it will pass away too. Selfishness cannot live forever. Self must perish because that is where that nature goes. Divine love sustains, because that is what it does. Jesus showed us that this world doesn't matter. Only being God's child matters. Only a life devoted to Divine Love matters. Only a life lived for God matters, because only God is forever.

Matthew 6:19–20
"Do not store up for yourselves treasures on earth, where moth and rust destroy, and where thieves break in and steal. [20] But store up for yourselves treasures in heaven, where moth and rust do not destroy, and where thieves do not break in and steal. (NIV84)

When I first became a believer, long before I knew anything, I used to read words like this and think that Jesus was just talking holy talk. I didn't understand at the time that everything that he said was the exact truth, and

nothing but the exact truth. Jesus wasn't kidding when he said anything. He spoke not one idle word, not one. Because I didn't actually believe him, the meaning of the words eluded me. I mean, I believed him, but in a way I didn't. I thought that he was talking the talk; do you understand what I am saying? I was a goober brain; I was a foolish goober brain, but eventually, slowly, I started to understand that he wasn't kidding about anything. To put this in Bible words, back then I sort of believed in him and now I totally believe in him. I now know that if the words come out of his mouth then they are the clear and absolute truth—period. I am still a goober brain, but not as foolish as I once was.

In the Bible, persons that understand the truth expressed in the Bible, live with an ability to see beyond what their eyes actually see. They see invisible things: attitudes, motives, responsibilities, duties and such. They see these things through the understanding that God has given them, and so they can avoid dangers and pitfalls. They have a light to guide them. Those people that know nothing of God, and his precepts and instructions, blindly walk through life until something or others fells them.

What I mean is this: There is a real eternal reality and there is an artificial temporary reality. The Bible reveals to you which is which, and how each operates. If you are connected to the Bible, then you can see the real reality for what it is, and you can also see the temporary reality and what it is about. This ability comes to you because you can see by the light of the truth that is in the Bible. If you don't have the Bible then you cannot see the truth, nor can you see a lie for what it is either. Those that do not have the Bible for a light are therefore in darkness. Because they live in darkness the fate of the world will overtake them and destroy them. This is unavoidable because they cannot see reality.

Life & Death

THE WORD LIFE DOESN'T REALLY mean the same thing in the Bible as it does in the world. The normal English word life is used as a metaphor, or as a simile, to describe real life. We all pretty much know the definition of what life is—right? To be alive is to be growing and living and existing and such, well it does mean pretty much the same in the Bible, except it means to be growing and living and existing inside of God.

Life as we think of it in the world is physical-universe life. You can see things that are alive. But, life as it is often referred to in the Bible is

a spiritual existence or relationship.

Life: definition - physical

an organismic state characterized by capacity for metabolism, growth, reaction to stimuli, and reproduction. (© Merriam-Webster, Incorporated)

I think that this is pretty much what I think of when I think of physical universe life, don't you?

Life: definition - spiritual

the state of being inside of God where God supplies the force to sustain your being.

Physical universe life is a matter of biology and spiritual life is a matter of being in a faith relationship with God.

I often find it very helpful to look at an opposite in order to understand a matter more fully. The opposite of life is death. To be dead is to in be a state where corruption eats away at what used to be you, until you no longer exist. We all know what happens to a member of the community that dies. That person is immediately removed from the society, never to return again. That definition might be a little insensitive but it is near the mark. Dead people are definitely excluded from the society. I mean, they cannot interact with or affect others directly in any meaningful way.

Spiritual death is very similar. A spiritually dead person is excluded from inside of God. That person is not spiritually sustained. They are like, say an arm that is cutoff from the body and falls to the ground. If one of your arms is cut off, there is a very short window of time where it might be reattached. If that window passes, then the arm has been corrupted and must be disposed of. As long as the arm is attached to your body, then it is supplied by the life of the body and it is so sustained.

Spiritual life is just like that. As long as you are part of God's body, you are sustained by his life force. Since God lives forever and ever, so do you. You are alive if you exist inside of God in this way.

Any being that removes themselves from God has become like that arm that was cut off. That person is no longer sustained by the body (God) and will decay in a state of ever increasing corruption.

When the Bible talks of life, it is usually talking about this spiritual state of life and not the physical biological life, so if you apply the physical definition to what is going on you might get confused.

Genesis 2:15–17
The Lord God took the man and put him in the Garden of Eden to work it and take care of it. 16 And the Lord God

> commanded the man, "You are free to eat from any tree in the garden; 17 but you must not eat from the tree of the knowledge of good and evil, for when you eat of it you will surely die." (NIV84)

This is an example of something being confusing if you apply the wrong definition of life. God told the man that if he ate from the forbidden tree that he would surely die. Notice that it says when you eat of it you will surely die. God told him that if he ate he would die then and there.

> **Genesis 3:2–5**
> The woman said to the serpent, "We may eat fruit from the trees in the garden, 3 but God did say, 'You must not eat fruit from the tree that is in the middle of the garden, and you must not touch it, or you will die.'
> " 4 "You will not surely die," the serpent said to the woman. 5 "For God knows that when you eat of it your eyes will be opened, and you will be like God, knowing good and evil."
> (NIV84)

This interchange is all about life and death. God told the man that if he ate, he would die, and the woman expanded that to mean that if they touched it they would die, but the important thing here is that Satan told the woman that God was lying and that she would surely not die, and she believed him.

Well, the story goes along and she and her husband did eat and they surely did die. But, the death that they experienced was not of the physical biological kind, no, it was of the spiritual disconnected kind. It was their relationship with God, the Sustainer, that was severed.

I don't believe that Satan himself knew that he was dead, any more than people walking around today know that they are dead. Satan and these walking dead people are selfish and only see themselves and do not understand the long term consequences of spiritual death.

Spiritual death is a dire thing. It is by far the worst thing that can happen to a being. It means that a person has been corrupted, separated from God, and has started the decaying process. They will progress in their corruption until there is nothing left. They are literally zombies but just don't know it yet. Remember that I am talking about spiritual death here and not physical death.

Life and death in the Bible is not quite that clear cut. Satan, and the fallen or dead angels, are eternally separated from God, and there is no remedy for them. They have broken the faith-bond with God, and have

started the decaying process. Nothing can be done for the spiritual beings that formally existed in heaven, but are now cut off from God. But for man, thankfully, this is not the case. For man, it is possible to be both alive, and to be dead, at the same time, because man has two natures. Man is both a physical universe being and he is also a spiritual heaven being. It is possible for the body to be spiritually dead but the spirit within to be spiritually alive.

Romans 8:10
But if Christ is in you, your body is dead because of sin, yet your spirit is alive because of righteousness. (NIV84)

See? The body is dead, and yet the spirit can be alive. This is why God created the physical universe in the first place. He wanted a place where his actual children (that are spirits like himself) could die spiritually, and then be brought back into a faith relationship with him, after they had seen, and learned, and understood, just what sin is, and what its eventual effect is. In the world you can look around and see the effect of sin, and you can read in the Bible and see what life truly is, and then you can decide that you do not want a life of death, but rather a life of life. That is the decision that you can make, and that ability is the entire reason for the physical universe. God built a life and death loophole into the legality of the physical universe. This loophole is one of many secrets that were hidden inside of God. Satan didn't see it and didn't expect it.

I don't believe that before the creation of the physical universe, that the angels in heaven with God could understand what death was. Before Satan rebelled and separated himself from God no one had ever died. I am sure that God told them that if they separated themselves from him that they would die, but who could have understood what that meant? What I mean is, that in an existence where no one has ever died, how can the inhabitants understand what death really means?

The physical universe was created so that life and death could be understood. We, who live in the world, surely know what it means to be dead. The angels in heaven can now look and see and comprehend also. We can learn the meaning of death, and we can learn its opposite- life. We can see and understand the outcome of death.

When you read in the book of Revelation, you can see just what spiritual death does to a world. The world goes insane, and everybody dies. That is what would have happened in heaven had God allowed death to remain there, but he didn't and he won't. Those that are spiritually dead

are excluded from heaven, and this is a very good thing for those that are alive. Would you really want to live in a place forever, where everyone goes more and more insane and brutally preys on one another, until everyone is destroyed? I think not. Well, it is impossible nonetheless. God is the Sustainer, he is Love, all that live in him are sustained in love and cannot go insane. Love is the power that brings harmony and it is a force that is eternal.

Whenever you see in the Bible talk concerning life and death please understand that it is most likely talking about spiritual life and spiritual death.

Eternal Life

OFTEN LIFE WITH GOD IS called eternal life. This is a good name, but if you don't understand what that means it can be misleading. It is evident in the Scriptures that spirit beings live forever. It is also evident that death does not exist in heaven.

The thing about eternal life is that it is not a long long time, not really. It is an existence apart from time. This can be a difficult thing for us to visualize. God can mosey along around the entire circumference of the earth at a leisurely pace, and not take any time doing it. If God were to walk the circumference of the earth in zero time, then you cannot say that he went very fast, because time is a factor of speed. Without time there is no speed, strange but true. The best way to describe it is to say that eternity is.

> **Exodus 3:13–14**
> **Moses said to God, "Suppose I go to the Israelites and say to them, 'The God of your fathers has sent me to you,' and they ask me, 'What is his name?' Then what shall I tell them?"** [14]
> **God said to Moses, "I AM WHO I AM. This is what you are to say to the Israelites: 'I AM has sent me to you.'"** (NIV84)

This seemingly strange name of God's is only strange when we consider time. God is saying that he is. For God, in eternity, is not then or when, but rather now. This is really mentally strange stuff. I can't say that I really understand it. God is, was, and will be, in our perspective, but he is always the I Am.

This is an important thing to understand however because for the most part the Bible prophecies are written without a time element. A single

sentence in the Bible might step over two thousand years without a blink. We shall see this later when we start looking at the prophecies. For now I would like you to just consider eternity as being a place without time.

I have noticed that while reading the prophecies with the understanding that for the most part time does not exist, a sequence of events is nonetheless maintained. For example: Satan elevated himself up above God and he was judged, event and result. But the time between these two events is impossible for us to determine because they both occurred in eternity.

Usually when the Bible talks about eternal life however, it is talking about living with God in eternity. The life in eternal life is what we talked about before, and that is in being in a harmonious relationship with God, as opposed to existing in a broken relationship apart from God. Eternal life means to live with God in eternity, that is, to live with him in heaven.

Sin

Chapter Three

T IS VERY IMPORTANT TO understand the concept of sin. People frequently think of sin as some action that is wrong, and is therefore sinful, and another action is right, and is therefore not a sin. This really isn't the best way to understand what sin is.

Sin is really anything that you might do for reasons other than it is what God would have had you do. Sin is mostly in our hearts and minds. The action that you do, or the event if you like, is not really the sinful thing, the sinfulness is found in your motives and reasons.

Romans 14:23

But the man who has doubts is condemned if he eats, because his eating is not from faith; and everything that does not come from faith is sin. (NIV84)

Everything that does not come from faith is sin. That is a very enlightening statement. If you know something is wrong, then it is wrong, even if it isn't wrong. If you do anything that you believe is wrong, even if is not really wrong, you commit sin, because what you really did was to break faith with God.

The key word in this is the word faith. If you are married and you flirt with someone other than your spouse, and you know in your heart that your spouse would not like it, then you have acted faithlessly toward your spouse, and have therefore sinned against your spouse. Can you see

just how subtle this can be? You might do something that no one in the whole world can see is sin but you know that it is. Conversely you can do something that everyone thinks is sinful, but for you it might not be sinful. This can get impossibly subtle and makes it completely impossible for a human to live without sinning. And also makes it impossible for one human to know the sin that others are doing. I am talking about disputable matters here. Some things are obviously sinful.

Romans 11:32
For God has bound all men over to disobedience so that he may have mercy on them all. (NIV84)

What an important Scripture to understand.

We are eternal spirit beings that God has placed into selfish bodies that have instincts (programming) that is contrary to a total faith relationship with God. It is impossible to have a totally committed relationship with God while you live in a human body. If nothing else you must eat and sleep. Now, my friends, remember that I am talking about very subtle things here. None of these things that I am now referring to will result in your being condemned. God knows that you live in such a body. The point here is not that you attain perfection but that you desire perfection.

Hebrews 5:7–10
During the days of Jesus' life on earth, he offered up prayers and petitions with loud cries and tears to the one who could save him from death, and he was heard because of his reverent submission. [8] Although he was a son, he learned obedience from what he suffered [9] and, once made perfect, he became the source of eternal salvation for all who obey him [10] and was designated by God to be high priest in the order of Melchizedek. (NIV84)

Jesus too lived in a human body. He too was subjected to its needs and drives, but as this passage says he reverently submitted to God, and prayed earnestly that God would save him from death. Wow.

Stop and ask yourself, why did Jesus go on a 40 day fast before starting his ministry? If you can answer that, then you have a very subtle understanding about what I am talking about.

My point is that no one is without sin. You, as long as you live in a human body, cannot go a day without committing some form of a selfish act. This fact is in no way an excuse for you to indulge in sinful acts. "I can't help that I am an alcoholic because I have the alcoholic gene." What nonsense. Everyone has the sin gene, everyone in a human body.

Our bodies are death, but we are not our bodies.

To better understand just what sin is we can look at its opposite. The opposite of sin is Divine Love. Divine Love always looks out for the betterment of the whole, and sin looks inward to the benefit of self. The body has many drives and they each nudge us into indulging them. The Spirit of God speaks to our spirit in a soft and gentle voice that directs us into acts that have no direct benefit to the body. Which voice do you obey? Since the Spirit directs us into actions that have no direct benefit to the flesh they must be obeyed in faith. The things that the body wants result in instant and immediate gratification and therefore do not require faith.

Matthew 6:2
"So when you give to the needy, do not announce it with trumpets, as the hypocrites do in the synagogues and on the streets, to be honored by men. I tell you the truth, they have received their reward in full. (NIV84)

Matthew 6:5
"And when you pray, do not be like the hypocrites, for they love to pray standing in the synagogues and on the street corners to be seen by men. I tell you the truth, they have received their reward in full. (NIV84)

Matthew 6:16
"When you fast, do not look somber as the hypocrites do, for they disfigure their faces to show men they are fasting. I tell you the truth, they have received their reward in full. (NIV84)

These three Scriptures illustrate the principle that if you do something for instant gratification then the gratification is what you get, but if you do something in faith then you will have come closer to God. Sin, however, can be very deceitful. We can do some 'selfless' act for one human, thinking that we are so good, and yet we did what we did because we found that person lovely to behold and so we secretly did what we did for selfish reasons. We might not consciously know what we did, or why we did it. Sin is a liar. A pretty girl smiles at us and so we give her what she wants, but a plain girl appeals to us and we ignore her, all without really knowing what we just did. Sin is so sneaky.

To grow in our relationship with God requires God to teach us these subtle things. We will be fooled by sin many times and God will many times show us the error. Growth takes time.

Hebrews 10:38–39
But my righteous one will live by faith. And if he shrinks
back, I will not be pleased with him."
³⁹ But we are not of those who shrink back and are de-
stroyed, but of those who believe and are saved. (NIV84)

A relationship with God is not about being sinless, but rather about staying the path, that is, in not shrinking back when we find things difficult, or when we don't get what we want. The attitude to have is the attitude that says, I will obey God even though I get nothing for it and even though I die in the attempt, because God is always right.

We are all in the same sin boat, so to say, so we should have compassion on our brothers and sisters who are also in the sin boat with us. I am not saying that we should forgive every sinner, but we should understand the deceitfulness of sin, and always keep in mind that we ourselves are saved only because of the mercy and love of God. And remember that no person, regardless of anything, is inherently better than any other. Our bodies don't mean a thing. Our status on the earth also doesn't mean a thing. Everything is about our faith relationship with God.

Nakedness

Chapter Four

Genesis 3:6-7
When the woman saw that the fruit of the tree was good for food and pleasing to the eye, and also desirable for gaining wisdom, she took some and ate it. She also gave some to her husband, who was with her, and he ate it. [7] Then the eyes of both of them were opened, and they realized they were naked; so they sewed fig leaves together and made coverings for themselves. (NIV84)

*E SEE HERE THE FALL* of man. Before sin was found in the man and woman they were perfectly holy and pure. The man and the woman had a perfect faith relationship with God. But after the fall they saw and understood the evil that they had done. The sin that they committed was visible to them, metaphorically. They were ashamed and tried to cover themselves. This, by the way, is a good thing. The first step to recovery with God is remorse and personal shame. This is the case because man is guilty of rebellion against God, after all.

This personal observation of their nakedness was symbolic of their awareness of their fallen state.

They did not expect this to happen. They didn't really understand what spiritual death was. When they saw the fruit of their actions, they were appalled. Their reaction to their exposure was exactly what is should have been, if they really wanted to get back with the Lord God.

Now, today, when people flaunt their sin, it is a very bad thing to do. Everyone will stumble in life but to brag about your sin and flaunt it is death. You would stand a better chance if you stood in a court room under indictment and told the judge what an ass he or she was. To see your sin and be ashamed and try to hide it means that you really want to be good, but the sin deceived you.

Hiding your nakedness is a very subtle thing. People are forever exposing themselves and saying (symbolically) look at me, I'm special, I matter.

The number one killer today (after the fall of man) is pride.

Proverbs 6:16–19
There are six things the Lord hates, seven that are detestable to him: [17] haughty eyes, a lying tongue, hands that shed innocent blood, [18] a heart that devises wicked schemes, feet that are quick to rush into evil, [19] a false witness who pours out lies and a man who stirs up dissension among brothers. (NIV84)

Number one on the list is haughty eyes or, said another way, pride. Pride takes many forms and we should take care to avoid it like the plague. The opposite of pride is humility. We are exhorted many times in the Bible to be humble. Pride thinks that what you think matters and humility knows that that we must be taught by God. People, every day, actually place themselves above God. It sounds silly when I say it that way, but it is nonetheless true. Anyone that is prideful has elevated themselves above God. Yikes!

Isaiah 5:21
Woe to those who are wise in their own eyes and clever in their own sight. (NIV84)

Relationships
Chapter Five

WHEN I SAY RELATIONSHIPS I mean formal relationships, that is, a meaningful relationship. You have a relationship with your spouse. You have relationships with your children or child. You have relationships with all of your relatives and close friends and such. I am talking about those kinds of relationships.

The ultimate relationship is one that you have with the Creator. He made you for that purpose and if you want to win the game of life you must have a meaningful and positive relationship with God.

There are two categories of people in the world today: Those that have a meaningful and positive relationship with God and those that don't. You can forget all other distinctions between people. This relationship with God category is the only one that counts.

Galatians 3:28
There is neither Jew nor Greek, slave nor free, male nor female, for you are all one in Christ Jesus. (NIV84)

Paul is talking to the Church in the passage. The Church is just a name for those that have a positive and meaningful relationship with God, through Jesus Christ. What this passage is saying is that if you belong to God because of your relationship with Jesus Christ then it doesn't matter what else you are or were. If you are connected to God in Christ then it doesn't matter if you are a Jew or a non-Jew, it doesn't matter if you were from the bottom of society or from the top, or if you are a man

or a woman.

The type of relationships I am talking about are those that exist between individual people. I am not talking about blood relationship, but rather personal relationships. Relationships can be good and they can be bad. A good relationship is characterized by a relationship whereby both parties care about the other and act in such a way as to make the relationship better. A bad relationship is characterized by one or both parties acting in such a way as to harm the other party. What makes a relationship good is faith, and conversely it is faithlessness that harms a relationship.

Faith is one of those words that people tend to give a religious meaning to that obscures the real meaning of the word. Faith toward God is exactly like faith between people in relationships. There is no difference at all. It is the same word and means the same thing. If you have faith that moves mountains it means that you have such a faithful relationship with God who can move mountains that if you need a mountain moved you know that he will move it for you. Faith is not a power that can move a mountain. God can move a mountain. If you are faithful in your relationship with God, then God will watch over you in everything and he will pave the way for you as you go through life. The faith is the same as the faith that you might have in your spouse, but because the faith is directed toward God then your expectations in the relationship are different than with your spouse.

What I mean, is that I might have faith in my dog, but I also know my dog. He is a dog after all. My realistic expectations are much different than the faith that I have in my wife. And also the faith I have in my God is much different than that I might have with my wife, because there is a huge difference between my God and my wife. Also, the Lord God Almighty has faith in me that is in keeping with my limitations.

Please don't turn faith into a religious word. Keep it real. Be faithful to God and to everyone else. It is important that you be faithful in all of your relationships because you cannot be unfaithful to a spouse, say, and yet be faithful to God. A faithful person is faithful. Become more faithful to the people around you and you will become more faithful to God.

Marriage

*I*T IS IMPORTANT TO UNDERSTAND that God made the world and everything in it, and that he made it to his exact specifications.

Some people imagine that God is like them, and that when he made the world it didn't come out exactly how he thought that it would. This is not true. The world is exactly how God expected it to come out. God plans what he is going to do to the exact degree and then he creates exactly that. If something is a certain way then God intended it to be that way.

We have a very simplistic idea of God and his creation. We make up stories for books, television or films where people have the ability to create things by magic. When I was a boy there were two shows on TV that I remember really liking: Bewitched and I Dream of Jeannie. On both of those shows the witch/genie would twitch a nose or cross her arms and blink and POW! There would be whatever they wanted. That is not how things work. That is kindergarten thinking.

If you really did have the power to create then you would have to know exactly what you were going to make, and exactly how you are going to make it. Imagine for example that you wanted to make a basketball. Now, stop and think: what would that require? How big does it have to be? Exactly. How thick is the rubber? And what kind of rubber? Exactly how many atoms does it take to make it, and which kinds, and how do you make them connect together? What did you make the atoms out of? Did you remember to put air in the ball? How much air? What pressure? This goes on and on and on. For our minds there is no end to the things that you must know before you can make anything. I am not exaggerating here, not one little bit. Look at this…

> **Luke 6:6–11**
> **On another Sabbath he went into the synagogue and was teaching, and a man was there whose right hand was shriveled. [7] The Pharisees and the teachers of the law were looking for a reason to accuse Jesus, so they watched him closely to see if he would heal on the Sabbath. [8] But Jesus knew what they were thinking and said to the man with the shriveled hand, "Get up and stand in front of everyone." So he got up and stood there. [9] Then Jesus said to them, "I ask you, which is lawful on the Sabbath: to do good or to do evil, to save life or to destroy it?" [10] He looked around at them all, and then said to the man, "Stretch out your hand." He did so, and his hand was completely restored. [11] But they were furious and began to discuss with one another what they might do to Jesus.** (NIV84)

Think about what is required to restore a shriveled hand. Jesus didn't just twitch his nose and blink and hope for the best. The power of God was

there, and God Almighty restored his hand with wisdom, understanding and knowledge. God grew whatever cells and such that were needed and straightened whatever bones were bent and did whatever else needed to be done to do this miracle. And God remembered to put life into the newly restored cells. God knew exactly what he was doing; do you, or can you?

My friend, think about this. Ponder it. Meditate on it and let it fill you. God is awesome.

Now, I have mentioned all of this about the exactness of God's creation so that you can understand that it is not an accident that God created man, male and female. He didn't have to do it that way. God could have done it any way he wanted, and so he did. He made man, male and female.

Genesis 1:27
So God created man in his own image, in the image of God he created him; male and female he created them. (NIV84)

We are created in the image and likeness of God, male and female. This doesn't mean that we look like God. It means that we are like God; our spirit natures are exactly like God, not our flesh and blood animal bodies. Inside we are like God. Outside we are male and female and we form relationships between us that are very much like the relationship with God that we should be forming.

The human relationship of husband and wife is as close to a relationship with God as you can get. The only relationship that is closer is the one that you can have with God directly through Jesus Christ the Bridegroom.

Ephesians 5:31–32
"For this reason a man will leave his father and mother and be united to his wife, and the two will become one flesh." *32 This is a profound mystery—but I am talking about Christ and the church.* (NIV84)

Verse 31 is a quote from Genesis that talks about the human union of marriage. And Paul says here that the marriage relationship is just like our union with God through Jesus Christ, and Paul also tells us that this is a profound mystery.

Can you see the symbolic nature in this? Much of the Bible is written this way. We see a marriage, and we then start filling in the blanks, as to what it all means, as we read the Bible.

In a marriage you have a man and a woman that both enter into a life-long bond of faith. They make a solemn vow before God that they will honor the union until death. They do this to form a family with which

to raise children.

When we look at a human marriage we should understand the symbolic nature of the union. The marriage symbolically represents the union of a spirit being (God) and a human being. The man represents God and the woman represents humanity. In the Bible whenever you see a male image it always represents a spirit being, such as God the Father, Jesus, the angels, and even Satan who is an angel also. If you see a female image then it is representing a human entity. I am talking about images here, and not individual people.

It should be understood that God is not actually a male, and human men are not more like God than women are. The point of this symbolism is not to make men think that they are better or higher than women, but rather so that we can learn our duties, and obey them, so that we can through our relationships learn more about God and his relationship with us. If a man marries a woman then he must give up his life and live for his wife, and she must do the same for her husband. When the couple has a child or children then their responsibilities include the children as well. Relationships are about responsibilities. The responsibilities that are incurred are lifelong. As a man lives for the benefit of his family he can better understand God's role toward us, and the same is true for the woman. Being faithful in your duties is to be faithful toward God and to learn about God's faithfulness toward us.

By the way, you should also understand that the angels that are represented as males are not actually males either. They are angels and as such have no sex. Angels do not reproduce.

Now, woman represents mankind, through which children are born. Women represent both men and women—symbolically. So, when a woman is married to a man it symbolically represents the union of a human-kind to the spirit-kind, that is, man to God, or God to man.

In the Bible, women play a more minor role than men, but this is only symbolic. Actually, men and women are completely and totally equal in the eyes of God. Inside they both have spirit selves that actually have no sex. Inside they are both the same; children of God, or I should say that they are sexless children of the sexless God.

God has laid out instructions concerning men in marriage and women in marriage so that though our obedience to God's instructions we can learn things about faithfulness which then relates to our relationship with

God. Everything in the Bible works exactly like this. When we obey what God tells us to do, then we learn some things about God. If we do not obey then we do not learn. Please don't think that God is on a power trip and that is why he wants you to obey him. It is always for your benefit that you should obey him. God is love and love is never on a power trip. Each and every thing that God tells you to do is for your benefit. You can do nothing for God. It is impossible for you to do anything for him. If you want to do something for God then love him, because that is what he wants. God loves you and he wants you to be with him in heaven and the way to do that is to develop a faithful relationship with him in love.

Union of Faith

HE UNION OF A MAN and a woman in marriage is more than anything else a union of faith, or a faith-union. Two people profess before witnesses that they will be one until death separates them. This is a solemn promise and this promise must not be violated. In fact no solemn promise can ever be broken without consequences. It is a vow made before God. Because this promise is made before God it is therefore a holy promise and the breaking of it will always carry heavy consequences. I see people breaking their holy vows all the time and then I see them complaining about the unfair God. ('If there is one,' they say.)

> **Matthew 19:3–12**
> **Some Pharisees came to him to test him. They asked, "Is it lawful for a man to divorce his wife for any and every reason?"**
> **⁴ "Haven't you read," he replied, "that at the beginning the Creator 'made them male and female,' ⁵ and said, 'For this reason a man will leave his father and mother and be united to his wife, and the two will become one flesh'? ⁶ So they are no longer two, but one. Therefore what God has joined together, let man not separate."**
> **⁷ "Why then," they asked, "did Moses command that a man give his wife a certificate of divorce and send her away?"**
> **⁸ Jesus replied, "Moses permitted you to divorce your wives because your hearts were hard. But it was not this way from the beginning. ⁹ I tell you that anyone who divorces his wife, except for marital unfaithfulness, and marries another woman commits adultery."**
> **¹⁰ The disciples said to him, "If this is the situation between a husband and wife, it is better not to marry."**
> **¹¹ Jesus replied, "Not everyone can accept this word, but**

only those to whom it has been given. [12] For some are eunuchs because they were born that way; others were made that way by men; and others have renounced marriage because of the kingdom of heaven. The one who can accept this should accept it." (NIV84)

This passage tells us a lot about marriage. The only permissible reason for a divorce is because of marital unfaithfulness, which is because if you are unfaithful in your marriage you have already broken the covenant that you had with your spouse. The act of marital unfaithfulness is a breaking of the covenant or vow.

I find it interesting that the disciples correctly interpreted this to mean that they cannot ever get a divorce and that Jesus agreed with them. The disciples then said that it would be better not to ever marry under those conditions, and Jesus again agreed with them, but then he pointed out that not everyone could forgo a sexual relationship. This tells us, by the way, that the highest or holiest relationship with God is one which you devote yourself to him and only to him, that is, you never marry, that is, you remain a virgin.

Now, understand that never marring is total abstinence, and not living with a person of the opposite sex outside of marriage. Biblically if you have sex with any person you have formed a marriage-like union with them. You have become one person with whom you have had sexual intercourse. Biblically, sexual intercourse is what consummates a marriage. A person that engages in sexual relations with persons not their wife or husband is called a fornicator and falls into the same category as murderers and such. My friend, you are called to be holy. God as permitted you to marry, if you want, but you must be faithful to the one that you marry. Faith is everything. I say this again, faith is everything. Now, we are all human and we have all made big mistakes. If you have done things in the past that have damaged your faith-union then repent of those things and do what you can to mend things. Always change your ways so as to make the faith-bond surer. Always change things to be a better wife or husband. As you improve in your interpersonal relationships you will grow closer to God. We are far from perfect, but we march on toward perfection.

Strangely this does not mean that you cannot get a divorce. If your spouse breaks the faith-bond then the faith-bond is broken. I have seen women stay with men that beat them because they believe that they cannot get a divorce, but this is not true. If your husband or wife beats

you, they have, by that action, already broken the bond of faith that may have existed between you. Anyway, I don't want to get into all of that, I just wanted to point that out for you.

When a man and a woman get married they stand in the presence of God and make a solemn vow—a confession of faith. Now, look at this passage...

Romans 10:8–10
But what does it say? "The word is near you; it is in your mouth and in your heart," that is, the word of faith we are proclaiming: ⁹ That if you confess with your mouth, "Jesus is Lord," and believe in your heart that God raised him from the dead, you will be saved. ¹⁰ For it is with your heart that you believe and are justified, and it is with your mouth that you confess and are saved. (NIV84)

This passage is talking about the confession of faith that bonds you to God through Jesus Christ. When you understand what Jesus did, and why he did it, and what it can mean to you, and then accept his sacrifice for yourself, and then make a public confession before God, then you have entered into a faith-bond with God that will last until either God dies (impossible), or you die (only if you break faith). This is why God is so against divorce. If you break faith with your husband or wife, you are also breaking faith with God, because you promised before God that you would not break faith—ever. This is serious stuff here.

What I am saying is that the only relationship possible between yourself and God is a relationship of faith. This relationship of faith is like any other relationship of faith. You are either faithful or you are not. You know when you are faithful and you know when you are not faithful. For you to be faithful to God you must be faithful in general, that is, faithful to those around you, such as to your spouse and/or children, your friends, your employer, your government, your whatever. Faithfulness is faithfulness. Any sin that you commit against a faith partner is a sin against God. If you are a father then you have a responsibility to your children and wife. If you are not faithful in your duties then you are unfaithful. Faithfulness is not fickle. You are either faithful or you are not. If you are not faithful then you had better examine yourself carefully and make whatever changes that are necessary. Your personal faithfulness is the most important quality that you have. Everything depends upon your faithfulness. In order to be faithful, you must put others before yourself. A faithful person puts the union above themselves. That doesn't mean giving in to your spouse in

everything. It means always doing the right thing with respect to your spouse or whomever you have a faith relationship with.

Children

UMAN CHILDREN ARE SYMBOLIC OF God's children, and they are actually God's children that have been entrusted into our care. That should raise a red flag as to the importance of how you care for them. They are God's children, yes, but they are also children in a fallen state and must be taught to be holy and just and everything else that God wants them to grow up to be. This is an awesome responsibility. However, leading your children to God is exactly that—leading. It is foolish to put a higher standard of obedience on your children than on yourself. If you yourself are living in a faithful relationship with God then you will lead your children along with you. All leadership works this way. The leader must lead. The leader must show the way. The leader must be the example.

One raises children up to their level, so to say. When you are being a faithful steward to your children, God will be with you, and will raise you up to his level. Always, and in every way, you must be the one that does the right thing. You should never expect others to change. You change. If you change in the right ways, then God will be with you and the others will follow you. If the others choose not to follow you, then their sin is on their own head. You must do the right thing. I am talking about very subtle things here.

What I am trying to say regarding children is that they are an awesome responsibility and also an awesome gift to you. They will give you many opportunities to grow in your obedience to God. When a person marries, their spouse becomes more important than themselves. When a couple has children, the children are more important than the parents. But that doesn't mean that you give the children everything that they may want: no, as in everything, this is far more subtle than that. Sometimes you must scold and rebuke, but also sometimes you must praise and embrace. Every child is different and every parent is different and every parent has a different spouse and in all of this you must do your faithful best. As you do your faithful best, God will cause you to grow in your knowledge and understanding of him. But that doesn't mean that you must marry and have children to grow in this knowledge and understanding because God has many other ways to teach you these things. If you choose the married life then you must be obedient to it.

Born Again

John 3:3
**In reply Jesus declared, "I tell you the truth, no one can see
the kingdom of God unless he is born again."** (NIV84)

E CAN SEE FROM THIS passage that to be born again is a very
important step. Jesus says here, that if you are not born again,
then you cannot even see the kingdom of God. To see the kingdom of
God, means that you have the Teacher inside of you illuminating the
meaning of the Scriptures to you. This is a very personal thing. The
key word here is see.

John 14:15–21
**"If you love me, you will obey what I command. [16] And I
will ask the Father, and he will give you another Counselor
to be with you forever— [17] the Spirit of truth. The world
cannot accept him, because it neither sees him nor knows
him. But you know him, for he lives with you and will be in
you. [18] I will not leave you as orphans; I will come to you.
[19] Before long, the world will not see me anymore, but you
will see me. Because I live, you also will live. [20] On that day
you will realize that I am in my Father, and you are in me,
and I am in you. [21] Whoever has my commands and obeys
them, he is the one who loves me. He who loves me will be
loved by my Father, and I too will love him and show myself to him."** (NIV84)

This passage says so much. If we really love Jesus, then we will listen
to him, that is, to the Bible, and do what he/it says. I don't mean that we
will do the parts that we think are right, but we will obey whatever he
says. This is very important. You might do 90% of what the Bible says,
because you agree with that 90% but then ignore 10% of it because you
don't want to do those things. People think that they are good people
because they do most of the Bible things, and those around them do not,
but that is not what constitutes obedience to God. God is to be obeyed
100%. So, this passage says that if you love Jesus then you will obey
him and because of this relationship that you now have with God through
Jesus Christ then Jesus will ask the Father on your behalf for him to give
to you a part of himself to live inside of you to act as a Teacher for you.

This is not something that happens in your mind. This is deeper than
that. This is something that happens in the core of your person, that is,
within your soul within the spirit you—the real you, the eternal you.

When Adam and Eve lived with God in the Garden before the fall

they had the Spirit of God living with them, inside of them. We can say that they were born of God. Remember the Scripture that says that God created them in his image and in his likeness. God is a spirit being and so were they. They had a living relationship with the Almighty, but then they sinned and the connection with God was broken. This is the meaning of the fact that they died then and there, in the Garden, after they sinned. Inside they were dead, and cut off from a living relationship with the Almighty. But then God told them what the result of their betrayal would be, and he then promised them that if they remained faithful, that he would send them a savior who would crush the head of Satan, and that they would be restored to a living state. This is why Adam at that time named his wife Eve, for she would be the mother of all of the living, spiritual living and not just animal physical life.

When Jesus died for us on the cross he defeated the Devil, and took from him the keys of death and made it possible for people to be alive again-inside, that is, he made it possible for people's spirit person within to be connectable to God the Holy Spirit from Heaven. This is incredibly important stuff here. To say that this is important is like saying that the sun is big and hot. The importance of the born-again union is truly beyond words.

John 17:6-8
"I have revealed you to those whom you gave me out of the world. They were yours; you gave them to me and they have obeyed your word. ⁷ Now they know that everything you have given me comes from you. ⁸ For I gave them the words you gave me and they accepted them. They knew with certainty that I came from you, and they believed that you sent me. (NIV84)

Look at what Jesus is saying here. Jesus came and did and said many things and the disciples who did not really understand the meaning of most of what he did and said nonetheless fully believed that God had sent Jesus to the earth to do and say them. The disciples believed that even though they did not fully understand the meaning of what Jesus did and said they nonetheless fully believed that each and every thing that Jesus said and did came directly from God. And because they believe in this way Jesus promised to send them the Teacher that would come and live within them. I know that my words are kind of going in circles here, but please bear with me and try to unwind them. Being in a faith relationship with God Almighty through Jesus Christ does not depend upon our understanding what Jesus said and did exactly. It depends upon

our believing in who and what Jesus is. If we believe that God sent Jesus to say and do what he did then we can receive his words and actions as having come from God. We can only do this if we accept the Bible in the same light as Jesus Christ himself. Then when we read the Bible we are receiving the very words of God. Our faith in this brings about an earth-shattering change in ourselves whereby we become actually reconnected to God by faith. This reconnection is called being born-again. The spirit within us, that became dead when Adam and Eve broke the faith-bond with God, becomes alive again by virtue of its reconnected state. It is like our cut-off spirit got grafted back into God. The spirit within us, that was dead because of its disconnected state, is reanimated because of its being reconnected to the Sustainer. That which was dead has been reborn, or born-again. Wow and double wow.

When a person that was dead inside becomes alive again, then God who now lives within that person starts revealing things to them. After you become born-again then when you read the Bible, you have your own personal Teacher living within you that reveals everything to you.

John 17:9, 20-26
⁹ I pray for them. I am not praying for the world, but for those you have given me, for they are yours.
²⁰ "My prayer is not for them alone. I pray also for those who will believe in me through their message, ²¹ that all of them may be one, Father, just as you are in me and I am in you. May they also be in us so that the world may believe that you have sent me. ²² I have given them the glory that you gave me, that they may be one as we are one: ²³ I in them and you in me. May they be brought to complete unity to let the world know that you sent me and have loved them even as you have loved me. ²⁴ "Father, I want those you have given me to be with me where I am, and to see my glory, the glory you have given me because you loved me before the creation of the world.
²⁵ "Righteous Father, though the world does not know you, I know you, and they know that you have sent me. ²⁶ I have made you known to them, and will continue to make you known in order that the love you have for me may be in them and that I myself may be in them." (NIV84)

Jesus not only was praying for his apostles, but he was praying for all of those that would believe in him through the apostles' words, that is, for you and for I also. Jesus is saying that for those that believe in him he would come and live inside of us just as the Father lived inside of him.

Wow, what a prayer and what an opportunity.

When we believe that God was in Jesus and that Jesus' words carry the authority of God Almighty, and we receive them as such, then a transformation occurs within us. That which was once separated from God, that is to say, dead, becomes a place that God can come inside of to live, and that place is therefore no longer dead, but alive again, thus born-again. Again, that is the meaning of being born-again.

John 3:4
"How can a man be born when he is old?" Nicodemus asked. "Surely he cannot enter a second time into his mother's womb to be born!" (NIV84)

In response to Jesus telling Nicodemus that he must be born again he said this. Nicodemus was thinking literal, but Jesus was talking about the spirit.

John 3:5–6
Jesus answered, "I tell you the truth, no one can enter the kingdom of God unless he is born of water and the Spirit. ⁶ Flesh gives birth to flesh, but the Spirit gives birth to spirit. (NIV84)

This is Jesus' answer to Nicodemus. He says that to be born the first time is the birth of the flesh, but the second birth is a spiritual rebirth. The spirit within man that was dead because of sin, that is, cut off from God, that is, a place where God could not live because of sin, now because of faith in what Jesus did on the cross, has become open to God's spirit and can receive his Spirit and in this way become spiritually alive again, or born again.

The born again experience is spiritual cleansing of the human soul that makes it possible for God to reconnect with a person, and through this reconnection, that person becomes alive again toward God and God becomes that person's God for real.

John 5:24
"I tell you the truth, whoever hears my word and believes him who sent me has eternal life and will not be condemned; he has crossed over from death to life. (NIV84)

Jesus speaks here in the past tense. Whoever hears Jesus' words and believes them as the words of God himself, that person has already crossed over from death to life. This is spiritual stuff here, not physical. Physically if you are reading this you are alive, right? But if you have crossed over from death to life you, who were once dead inside because

of sin, have become alive because of your faith in the Son of God. That is, your faith connection to God has been restored. Everything, and I mean everything, is about your connection to God. Nothing else matter in the world—period.

Mark 8:36
What good is it for a man to gain the whole world, yet forfeit his soul? (NIV84)

Baptism
Chapter Six

Christian Baptism

CHRISTIAN BAPTISM IS CONNECTED TO the born-again experi-ence. There were really only two things that the biblical Chris-tians ritually observed: baptism and communion. Both are sym-bolic expressions of spiritual truths.

Romans 6:3–4
Or don't you know that all of us who were baptized into Christ Jesus were baptized into his death? ⁴ We were there-fore buried with him through baptism into death in order that, just as Christ was raised from the dead through the glory of the Father, we too may live a new life. (NIV84)

When a person first comes to Christ they are spiritually dead, they must acknowledge this fact and understand that they must die to the world before they can be reborn in Christ and so they are ritually buried into the earth through baptism, then they are united to Christ in his death and finally are ritually resurrected with Christ Jesus through Christ's resur-rection and so come up out of the waters of baptism. This is the meaning behind Christian baptism.

Baptism is an acknowledgement of what you are professing. You are

saying to the world that you are dead to the world, but alive again in Christ through his resurrection. The born-again experience technically or ritualistically occurs while you are submerged under the water. At that point in the event, you who were dead have life enter into you, that is the Holy Spirit enters into you, and this life in you reanimates your spirit to new life in Christ. Being now alive, that is, born-again in Christ, you are then resurrected up out of the water to live as one now belonging to Christ Jesus, that is, one being in a marriage-like faith-bond with Jesus Christ.

Baptism is only a symbolic expression of this invisible spiritual event.

John's Baptism

HRISTIAN BAPTISM IS A DIFFERENT thing John's baptism. In John's baptism, a person was ritually cleansed from his sin, so that he or she could start over before God. It had nothing to do with death and resurrection. Both baptisms dealt with the sin problem, but in quite different ways. John's cleaned you from past sins by faith and Jesus' gave you a new life. John was a prophet of God and as such he was God's representative and when he then baptized a person to clean away their past sins the person could put their faith in this fact. The people believed in John and therefore they believed that God would forgive them their past sins through this baptism.

It is important to understand that neither baptism really did anything. Both were symbolic expressions for you, so that you could put your faith in God. What I mean is anyone could have been baptized but it means nothing unless the person entered into the event in faith. It was the faith in God that saved them, then as it is today.

Moses' and Joshua's Baptisms

T IS NOT COMMONLY UNDERSTOOD that both Moses and Joshua baptized Israel in a symbolic way.

1 Corinthians 10:2
They were all baptized into Moses in the cloud and in the sea. (NIV84)

The whole story of Moses and the liberation of Israel is a symbolic one. The people of Israel represent the Children of God, that is, the body of believing humans, or those that have a covenant with God, that is, those that have relationship with God. Egypt is symbolic of the world, or those

that do not have a relationship with God. So, we see that the whole body of believers was being held captive in the world, much like they are today, and so God sent to them a deliverer; Moses, who is symbolic of Christ Jesus the Redeemer and Savior.

Moses was chosen by God, like Jesus. He was sent to deliver the believers, like Jesus. He was rejected by those that should have welcomed him, and he therefore went away, all just like Jesus. While away from Israel he took a wife of foreign birth, (Jesus and the Gentiles). Then, at the time ordained by God, he returned and destroyed the symbolic world (Egypt) while saving the Israelites, just like in the book of Revelation. The whole story is symbolic of what is yet to occur. The whole Egypt-Moses-Israelites story is a shadow of what will soon come upon the whole world.

In the case of Moses, he gathered up the body of believers out of the 'world' and took them through the waters of baptism (death) on toward the Promised Land (heaven). But, Moses was unable to bring them to the Promised Land because he himself was guilty of sin, but Christ Jesus, the sinless one, entered into real death and was really resurrected to everlasting life and so he is really able to save us forever. Moses is a shadow and Jesus is the real deal. Everything in the Bible ultimately points to Jesus Christ.

The Bible frequently foretells future events through symbolic events in the Old Testament.

In the case of Joshua we see the man with the same name as Jesus (which means Savior) and he too baptizes the body of believers through a miraculous passing through water and takes them to the Promised Land which is again a symbolic heaven. So, we see that Joshua is a shadow of Jesus also.

You must always keep your eyes open for symbolic words and events when reading the Bible. When you see them they make the story make sense. Until you see the symbolisms you are just reading an interesting story, but when you see the story behind the story you begin to see and understand what God is doing.

Baptism is a very important event in the Bible and you should endeavor to understand all aspects of it. As Christians, that is, as those that have the Teacher within them, we should understand the meaning of what we are reading, and we should understand the deeper reasons for why things in the Bible are the way they are. My deeper understanding of baptism

shows me more clearly that I have died to the world and that I live for God in Christ. I live for the promised City that is above and not for anything that this culture might have to offer me. There are things here that catch my eye from time to time, but then I remember what is really going on and I keep myself on the correct path.

Heaven, Hell & World
Chapter Seven

EAVEN IS THE "UNIVERSE" IN which God lives. It is a universe that is fundamentally different than the physical universe. There is no time in heaven and this tells us that it is then not made up of energy and/or matter as the physical universe is. God is everywhere in heaven and in fact everything in heaven is more or less within God.

There are three forces here that really come from heaven and they are Love, Faith and Hope. These three are spiritual forces and not forces of the mind nor do they find any counterpart in the natural world.

1 Corinthians 13:13
And now these three remain: faith, hope and love. But the greatest of these is love. (NIV84)

The fact that these three remain is due to the fact that they are eternal. If they are eternal then they do not come from the natural universe, which is only temporary and can only produce temporary things.

The love that this is talking about is not romantic love, but Divine Love. The definition of Divine Love can be found in 1 Corinthians 13:1-8. We were created by God to intuitively understand these three forces. Of all the creatures of the earth, only man can understand these three forces.

All beings that live in heaven are beings of love, faith and hope. It is impossible to live in heaven and not be a being of love, faith and hope.

Love is the force that defines heaven. God is Love[1]. Every being in heaven is connected to God by faith. Every being in heaven has faith in Divine Love. Any being that loses their faith in Divine Love finds themselves separated from God. Faith is broken between a being and God when that being elevates themselves above Divine Love, that is, they have faith in themselves. In your own soul either God is supreme or you hold yourself superior to God, that is, you hold yourself above Divine Love, that is, you hold yourself as being more important than the good of all. When you hold yourself as being more important than God, that is, Divine Love, then you have broken your faith-bond with God and it becomes impossible for you to live in union with God. Since God is the whole of the universe of heaven, a being that has broken their connection with God must live in a godless place, that is, in a place in which God is not.

Biblically speaking the godless place has a name and is called Hell. That is what Hell is. Hell is a universe where Divine Love is not the force that defines it. Hell is defined by its very godless nature. Hell is the place in which its inhabitants are each guided by what they think and want. Hell's inhabitants do not embrace Divine Love, but rather their own desire.

Sin is symbolically represented in the Bible as fire. Hell is not literally a place of fire, but rather is a place where sin reigns. Sin is like a fire that consumes the forest. Sin is like a fire that consumes its hosts. Because Hell is not defined by Divine Love it is a place of self-consumption. It is the very nature of sin to consume. It is the very nature of Divine Love to sustain. Symbolically, Hell is represented as a place of fire, and Heaven is represented as a place with clouds which bring the sustaining rains. These are only symbols, neither is literal.

The Earth is a place that is more or less between Heaven and Hell. The Earth is a place where its habitants can be either beings of Divine Love or beings of Self, Sin if you prefer. Earth is a place where it is possible for both natures to exist. There can be no being of Divine Love in Hell and neither can there be beings of self-interest in heaven, both are impossible.

Man is a being of Earth. As the Earth has two natures, so man has two natures. Man can be selfish on the outside but selfless on the inside, within the spirit person or soul.

Here on Earth one can taste Divine Love or sinful self-interest. Here on Earth one can choose which to put one's faith in. One can choose to put one's faith in oneself, or one can choose to put one's faith into Divine

---

1)   1 John 4:8

Love.

The physical universe is a temporary place where God is teaching man and the angels (who are watching) the result of self-interested faith or Divine-interested faith.

> **Deuteronomy 30:19–20**
> **This day I call heaven and earth as witnesses against you that I have set before you life and death, blessings and curs-es. Now choose life, so that you and your children may live ²⁰ and that you may love the LORD your God, listen to his voice, and hold fast to him. For the LORD is your life, and he will give you many years in the land he swore to give to your fathers, Abraham, Isaac and Jacob.** (NIV84)

When you read through the Bible you must pay attention to the symbolic representations of each of these places; they are everywhere.

Egypt, Assyria, Babylon & Israel

Chapter Eight

GYPT, ASSYRIA AND BABYLON ARE each symbols of the world system as a whole. The Bible is written in such a way that the whole biblical world is symbolic for the whole actual world. The biblical world is a miniature world. Within the biblical world you find people that obey God and those that do not obey God; you find people that are in a covenant relationship with God and those that are not in a covenant relationship with God.

Each of these three symbolic worlds oppressed the children of God. In the case of Egypt, the deliverance of the children of God by Moses was a very visible and definite event. In the case of Egypt, a deliverer of God came and destroyed the "world" and gathered up the children of God and brought then toward the Promised Land (symbolic for heaven). The people during Moses' time were not ready to enter into heaven and so, because of sin, they all died in the desert, but their children were later brought into the Promised Land by yet another deliverer by the name of Jesus, that is, Joshua which is the same name as Jesus but in the Hebrew. The "world" was devastated just before the children of the promise were gathered. This is exactly the scenario that will take place at the Second Coming of the Lord.

Whereas Egypt depicts the whole scenario of the end times, the Assyrian empire does not. The nation of Israel, that is, the ten northern tribes of Israel, were from the conception of the nation in rebellion against God. After King Solomon rebelled against God, God took most of the nation away from his son. Ten of the twelve tribes rebelled against the king and formed their own nation. This nation was in direct rebellion against God. God sent the nation of Assyria against them and sometime around 700 BC the peoples of the nation of Israel were defeated by the Assyrians and the survivors were carried off into captivity into the north. The descendants of these Israeli survivors are still there. There are myths today that speak of the lost 10 tribes, but they are not lost and will be gathered up with the scattered descendants of descendants of Judah just after the Second Coming of the Lord. At the time of the Second Coming of the Lord, all the descendants of Jacob will be gathered up from all around the world and be reestablished by God in the Promised Land.

Sometime around five or six hundred years before Jesus' birth the Babylonian empire came to Judah (the two remaining tribes) and totally destroyed the city of Jerusalem and all of the Jewish cities and carried off the people into captivity to Babylon. The people were held in Babylon as second-class citizens and remained there for 70 years. After 70 years, some of the descendants of the captives returned to the Promised Land, but most did not return and remained scattered throughout the symbolic world.

The descendants that returned to the Promised Land comprised a symbolic restoration of the people. This restoration was only a symbolic restoration. The real restoration is the restoration that will occur just after the Second Coming of the Lord.

Matthew 23:37
"O Jerusalem, Jerusalem, you who kill the prophets and stone those sent to you, how often I have longed to gather your children together, as a hen gathers her chicks under her wings, but you were not willing. (NIV84)

The people of the covenant were still in rebellion at the time of the First Coming of the Lord. The events of the book of Revelation will be directed against the descendants of Israel and will serve to purge all sin from the people so that at the Second Coming they will be ready to be gathered and established in the Land.

I will be examining all of this in much more detail as this book progresses. For now I just want you to understand that most of the events in the Old Testament are symbolic of the real event of Revelation. I am

summarizing when I say Revelation because there are prophecies all over the Bible that talk about what is happening in Revelation. There is nothing in the book of Revelation after the third chapter that has been fulfilled yet. Almost everything in that book will be fulfilled during a seven-year period just before the Gathering of Israel.

We can, by looking at the past events, learn a great deal of detail concerning the events of Revelation. The events of ancient Egypt, Assyria and Babylon all give important clues concerning the things that are yet to happen. They are all shadows of the real event.

There are really only two groups of people in the world; those that have faith in God and those that do not have faith in God. Of those that have faith in God we have the Church and all the others, which is almost totally the descendants of Israel. So, in a way, we have three groups of people: Church, Jews and Gentiles.

The Bible has things to say to each of these three groups. It is important to understand which group is being referred to. Something said to the Church might not apply to the Israelites. Something said to the Israelites might not apply to the Gentiles. And something said concerning the Gentiles might not apply to either body of believers. Everything in the Bible has a context and the context must be understood.

When you read in the Bible something about Egypt it is usually the whole world of Gentile people that are really being talked about. We will talk about this later but for now I would like to point out that when the children of Israel went to Egypt at the time of Joseph and subsequently became slaves, this is an image of the world right now. The Roman army totally defeated Israel and scattered the Jews throughout the entire known world and they have been in the world ever since. The Jews have been persecuted everywhere they have gone. This is just what happened in Egypt all those years ago. At the time of Moses, Moses was sent by God to deliver the children of Israel from the persecution, and while doing that, God destroyed Egypt. This is just a preview of what his going to happen to the whole world very soon.

Everything in Bible history is about the fall and restoration of man—everything. There is nothing significant in history other than that. There is nothing that is going to happen in the world that is not about the fall and restoration of man. The world and everything in it belongs to God and he will do with it what he wants. He has established a plan and that plan marches on with totally precise steps. The world has its own history,

but it is a useless history because it doesn't work with God's plan. More on this later, for now please understand that the Bible, from beginning to end, is about the fall and restoration of man; all of it, every part of it. That is what the Bible is about, and that is what the world is about. This is what makes understanding the Bible so very important. Studying world history without an intimate knowledge of God and his plan is just spinning your wheels. The world may honor you for your understanding of world history, but it is useless in saving your spiritual life.

Potter

Chapter Nine

POTTER IS A PERSON THAT forms clay into useful objects, such as bowls and cups and such. The Bible symbolically calls God the Potter as he forms from "the dust of the ground" vessels useful to himself, that is, he made man and he works through people to bring about his will on the earth.

Genesis 2:7
...the Lord God formed the man from the dust of the ground and breathed into his nostrils the breath of life, and the man became a living being. (NIV84)

The Bible poetically says that we were made out of dust, or earth. God made us so. This is literally true as our bodies are made out of the atoms that make up the earth. The Potter made us out of clay, if you like. He made our bodies out of dust and then (and this is very important) he breathed into the earthen vessel a breath from himself, that is a part that is not of this creation, and in this way the earthen man became a living soul; a spirit being that was like God. Imagine this. Think about this; the Potter through his own act and desire made what he wanted to make for his own purposes. Every single person was created by God. Every single person belongs to God. Whether you know it or not, or whether or not you even believe it, you were put on this earth by the Potter.

Isaiah 29:16
You turn things upside down, as if the potter were thought

to be like the clay! Shall what is formed say to him who formed it, "He did not make me"? Can the pot say of the potter, "He knows nothing"? (NIV84)

Now, you must read this, understanding the symbolism. The Potter is God and the pot is a person. Is a person that is made out of dust like the one that made him or her? Can a pot make the potter; can a person make God? Does the pot know anything compared to the potter; can any person know more than God about anything? Can a person say that God did not make him or her? If he or she does say this then what a joke this is to the watching spirit beings. Is it wise for a person to criticize God, or to suggest that he or she knows better than God? You must read the symbolism.

Isaiah 64:8
Yet, O Lord, you are our Father. We are the clay, you are the potter; we are all the work of your hand. (NIV84)

Understanding this relationship is just about the first thing that a person must understand. To sit around and complain about your lot and the injustice in the world is just unproductive foolishness. If you don't like your lot then draw closer to the Potter and let him form you into something more useful for noble purposes.

2 Timothy 2:20–21
In a large house there are articles not only of gold and silver, but also of wood and clay; some are for noble purposes and some for ignoble. [21] If a man cleanses himself from the latter, he will be an instrument for noble purposes, made holy, useful to the Master and prepared to do any good work. (NIV84)

The Lord God has expectations for you. He formed you from the dust of the earth and breathed into you the spirit of life and in this way you became a god-child-like person. You have potential, but you are not left to your own resources, but rather God desires to work with you, and in you, and through you, to work his own good purposes. You can rebel against this destiny or you can willingly get on board. What you will choose to do is up to you.

The teeny tiny gentle little person that is deep within you is the person that must turn to God. The motivation of such a turn has nothing to do with pride or status or self-anything. The spirit you within, your soul, must command quiet from the rest of you. In this time of quiet and patience you allow God to direct you. This is called prayer. During prayer you don't let your mind take control and spill out a list of worldly desires, but

rather you quiet your mind and listen to peace gently guide and point you. This is all so subtle that it is like the puff of a butterfly's wings; gentle quiet patience and the guidance of the Spirit of the Bible to show you the way. As you bask in the Spirit of the Lord he can gently reform you into a different sort of person; a person that belongs to him and is reformed into his image and likeness. As you pray embrace gentleness and peace; embrace kindness and love; embrace joy and patience; embrace goodness and self-control; embrace God.[1]

---

1) Galatians 5:22-23

Sea & Islands
Chapter Ten

✿

A *VERY COMMON SYMBOL OR IMAGE* in the Bible is the image of a sea. The sea frequently refers to a great many people. The idea is that when you look at a whole mass of humanity you don't really see the individuals, rather you see the movement of the whole sea. If the sea is calm, then the people are at peace. If the sea is raging, then the people as a whole are in turmoil. When the wind blows on the sea to whip it into a rage, then this means that spiritual forces are working on the sea to make it do things. Wind is symbolic of spiritual forces as they are invisible and we cannot see where they come from or where they are going but they do affect things profoundly. As an individual, you do not have to rage and froth with the sea. As an individual, you can choose peace. Peace between you and the Lord God, that is, not peace for the world.

Isaiah 17:12
Oh, the raging of many nations— they rage like the raging sea! Oh, the uproar of the peoples— they roar like the roaring of great waters! (NIV84)

This is how we learn the meaning of the Bible's images. Isaiah tells us directly that the raging sea is symbolic of many raging nations.

Revelation 4:6
Also before the throne there was what looked like a sea of glass, clear as crystal. In the center, around the throne, were four living creatures, and they were covered with eyes, in front and in back. (NIV84)

Sea and Islands

Here we see a very calm sea and it represents people, or beings, in heaven before the throne of God. It is not surprising that the sea here in heaven is calm like glass.

Now, when we look out upon the great sea we might see some islands. The islands are symbolic of nations, that is, defined clumps in the sea.

Isaiah 40:15
Surely the nations are like a drop in a bucket; they are regarded as dust on the scales; he weighs the islands as though they were fine dust. (NIV84)

Here we see that the nations are called islands and that God is affected by the nation's opinions like dust might affect the scale you might use at the grocery store. Do you consider the dust that might be on the grocery store scale as to how it might affect the price of the produce? That is how much God is affected by the notions of the nations. But, that doesn't mean that God is not affected by his children. Look at this.

James 5:16
The prayer of a righteous man is powerful and effective.
(NIV84)

God makes a distinction between the sea in general and his beloved children.

The world shakes its fist at God and rants about what is fair and right, but God does not listen. He knows what is fair and right and will do exactly that.

These symbolic images that I have been talking about are found throughout the prophetic passages of the Bible, and we will look at them in context as we progress through this book.

There are many more images in the Bible and I will mention those I think appropriate as we look at those Scriptures.

Time
Chapter Eleven

*I*N HEAVEN THERE IS NO time. I don't mean to say that it lasts for a very long time, no, there is no time—none. Time does not exist in eternity. This is a difficult concept for us time-people to grasp. A person in heaven could sit down and hand-copy every book ever written on earth and take no earth time doing it; mind-boggling. Understanding eternity is like understanding the extent of God—not possible.

Let us look at an example of how time is treated in the Bible.

Malachi 3:1–4
"See, I will send my messenger, who will prepare the way before me. Then suddenly the Lord you are seeking will come to his temple; the messenger of the covenant, whom you desire, will come," says the Lord Almighty. ² But who can endure the day of his coming? Who can stand when he appears? For he will be like a refiner's fire or a launderer's soap. ³ He will sit as a refiner and purifier of silver; he will purify the Levites and refine them like gold and silver. Then the Lord will have men who will bring offerings in righteousness, ⁴ and the offerings of Judah and Jerusalem will be acceptable to the Lord, as in days gone by, as in former years. (NIV84)

The first thing we see is a prophecy of the coming of John the Baptist (God's messenger) who we are told in the Gospels was sent to prepare the way for Jesus. But, then, in the very next sentence we see that this

prophecy is talking about the Second Coming of Christ and not the First. When Jesus comes the Second time it will be during the events recorded in the book of Revelation. The Second Coming is a great judgment. "Who can endure the day of his coming?," the above passage says. This is the Great and Terrible Day of the Lord. We will be looking at all of this in great detail later, but for now I just want you to notice that this prophecy hops over two thousand years in a single bound. The prophecies can be like that. We have to read them carefully and understand them with wisdom. Before you can read them correctly with confidence you have to know the major events in the plan. When you understand the plan and its events, you can then understand the prophecy.

Clouds
Chapter Twelve

LOUDS ARE SYMBOLIC OF THE spirit beings from heaven.
Daniel 7:13
"In my vision at night I looked, and there before me was one like a son of man, coming with the clouds of heaven. (NIV84)

Job 20:6–7
Though his pride reaches to the heavens and his head touches the clouds, 7 he will perish forever, like his own dung; those who have seen him will say, 'Where is he?' (NIV84)

Here Zophar is speaking of man. He says that man is so filled with pride that his head touches the clouds, meaning that man thinks that he knows things like the angels of God do. Man rises himself up to their level but he really knows nothing.

In Scriptures like these you must interpret them understanding the symbolic nature of the words.

1 Thessalonians 4:13–18
Brothers, we do not want you to be ignorant about those who fall asleep, or to grieve like the rest of men, who have no hope. 14 We believe that Jesus died and rose again and so we believe that God will bring with Jesus those who have fallen asleep in him. 15 According to the Lord's own word, we tell you that we who are still alive, who are left till the coming of the Lord, will certainly not precede those who

have fallen asleep. [16] For the Lord himself will come down from heaven, with a loud command, with the voice of the archangel and with the trumpet call of God, and the dead in Christ will rise first. [17] After that, we who are still alive and are left will be caught up together with them *in the clouds* to meet the Lord in the air. And so we will be with the Lord forever. [18] Therefore encourage each other with these words. (NIV84)

This passage is talking about when Jesus will come back to earth to gather up his body, the Church, before the Great and Terrible Day of the Lord. This is commonly referred to as the Rapture. I like that word rapture and think that it describes this event very well so I use it as a reference.

What I want you to see now is that Jesus is going to bring with him those Christians that have died before this event, and they are depicted here as clouds.

Whenever you see the word cloud or clouds in the Bible take special note to see if it is being used metaphorically.

Desert

Chapter Thirteen

DESERT OFTEN REFERS TO A place where there is little or no understanding of the Word of God.

Psalm 1:3
He [a man that reads, knows and obeys the Bible] is like a tree planted by streams of water, which yields its fruit in season and whose leaf does not wither. Whatever he does prospers. (NIV84)

This describes the opposite, that is, a man who follows the God through the Word.

Isaiah 40:3
A voice of one calling: "In the desert prepare the way for the Lord; make straight in the wilderness a highway for our God. (NIV84)

Here we see a prophecy about John the Baptist. It says that he is calling in the desert, but this is not a literal desert. It means that he is talking to a people that do not understand the Bible.

Isaiah 41:17–20
"The poor and needy search for water, but there is none; their tongues are parched with thirst. But I the Lord will answer them; I, the God of Israel, will not forsake them. ¹⁸ I will make rivers flow on barren heights, and springs within the valleys. I will turn the desert into pools of water, and the parched ground into springs. ¹⁹ I will put in the desert

**the cedar and the acacia, the myrtle and the olive. I will
set pines in the wasteland, the fir and the cypress together,
[20] so that people may see and know, may consider and understand, that the hand of the Lord has done this, that the
Holy One of Israel has created it.** (NIV84)

This is a prophecy concerning the Millennial Kingdom Age, that is,
the time during which Satan is bound in hell and the will of God is done
on earth as it is in heaven. We see that the Bible is using imagery here
to tell us what it will be like. You must read passages like this with the
understanding that the words are not just literal words but carry spiritual
meaning too. In the world which has been like a desert, God will cause
his truth to become available, that is water from springs, and the result
will be plenty of spiritual growth.

Ezekiel 20:35
**I will bring you into the desert of the nations and there,
face to face, I will execute judgment upon you.** (NIV84)

This passage is talking about the period of time that we are now in. The
Israelites have been cast out of the 'fruitful land' and find themselves in
the nations that do not know the Word of God, that is, the Gentile nations.

When you understand the imagery of the Bible, the Bible stops being
a confusing book and starts becoming a fascinating book.

During this book I will show you many more symbolic words in context.
I will point them out and then you will see what I mean.

The Shadow Shows
Chapter Fourteen

NE OF MY FAVORITE SYMBOLIC words in the Bible is the word shadow. We all know what a shadow is, but the Bible frequently uses it metaphorically. Imagine that there is a man standing outside but you cannot see the man but you can see his shadow. You can look at the shadow and see that it is a man. You can get some idea of the size of the man and his clothes and such. You might, or might not, see other things in the shadow, but the point is, is that you do not see the man in the shadow but only the shadow.

When the Bible uses a shadow of an event, what we see is usually a smaller version of the real event and when we look at it we can see some things that tell us of the real event. Shadows in the Bible work in reverse time, that is, the shadow appears before the real event.

There are many shadows in the Old Testament.

Job 12:22
He reveals the deep things of darkness and brings deep shadows into the light. (NIV84)

We have seen that light represents truth, especially truth that has been revealed in the Bible so that we can see and understand it. And darkness is a place where we cannot see the truth unless God shines his light on it. And a shadow is a place where we can almost make out the truth because God's light is shining nearby.

Colossians 2:16–17
Therefore do not let anyone judge you by what you eat or drink, or with regard to a religious festival, a New Moon celebration or a Sabbath day. [17] These are a shadow of the things that were to come; the reality, however, is found in Christ. (NIV84)

This is one of my favorite passages. All of the things that were done under the Old Covenant were shadows of the reality that Christ would bring to light. It is not that the things in the Law were not true, but rather that they had to be spiritually discerned and that discernment comes by the Spirit of Christ. To go through the motions of religious observance has little benefit. To understand the truth behind them is of great value. These things were shadows of the truth; only shadows. In Christ the Spirit of God reveals to us the reality of them.

Let us take a look at Moses and Jesus. Moses was a shadow of Christ.

Exodus 1:22–2:2
[22] Then Pharaoh gave this order to all his people: "Every boy that is born you must throw into the Nile, but let every girl live."
[1] Now a man of the house of Levi married a Levite woman, [2] and she became pregnant and gave birth to a son. When she saw that he was a fine child, she hid him for three months. (NIV84)

Pharaoh was Satan's man and in that capacity he issued an order to kill all of the Israelite baby boys.

Matthew 2:16
When Herod realized that he had been outwitted by the Magi, he was furious, and he gave orders to kill all the boys in Bethlehem and its vicinity who were two years old and under, in accordance with the time he had learned from the Magi. (NIV84)

Herod too was Satan's man and he too sought to kill the Lord's child. But, as we know, God brought both Moses and Jesus through the danger to life.

Both Jesus and Moses were special children sent from God to deliver the children of Israel.

Now remember, you have to interpret the Old Testament stories to understand their meaning. In the book of Acts, Stephen, while talking to the Jewish elders, pointed out to them the fact that Moses was like

Jesus in that he had been sent by God to deliver the people but was at first rejected by the people.

> **Acts 7:20–29**
> "At that time Moses was born, and he was no ordinary child. For three months he was cared for in his father's house. [21] When he was placed outside, Pharaoh's daughter took him and brought him up as her own son. [22] Moses was educated in all the wisdom of the Egyptians and was powerful in speech and action.
> [23] "When Moses was forty years old, he decided to visit his fellow Israelites. [24] He saw one of them being mistreated by an Egyptian, so he went to his defense and avenged him by killing the Egyptian. [25] Moses thought that his own people would realize that God was using him to rescue them, but they did not. [26] The next day Moses came upon two Israelites who were fighting. He tried to reconcile them by saying, 'Men, you are brothers; why do you want to hurt each other?'
> [27] "But the man who was mistreating the other pushed Moses aside and said, 'Who made you ruler and judge over us? [28] Do you want to kill me as you killed the Egyptian yesterday?' [29] When Moses heard this, he fled to Midian, where he settled as a foreigner and had two sons. (NIV84)

Jesus, like Moses, when he came to deliver the people, was rejected by the people and so, for a time, he went away.

> **Luke 19:11–15**
> While they were listening to this, he went on to tell them a parable, because he was near Jerusalem and the people thought that the kingdom of God was going to appear at once. [12] He said: "A man of noble birth went to a distant country to have himself appointed king and then to return. [13] So he called ten of his servants and gave them ten minas. 'Put this money to work,' he said, 'until I come back.'
> [14] "But his subjects hated him and sent a delegation after him to say, 'We don't want this man to be our king.'
> [15] "He was made king, however, and returned home. (NIV84)

I find it interesting that Moses took a wife among the Gentiles while he was away and symbolically so did Jesus, for the Church went to the Gentiles after the Jews rejected it. Interesting things can be found in the Bible.

The parallels of Moses and Jesus with respect to the deliverance of the children of Israel are very important for us to see and understand. Moses

came and with one plague after another devastated Egypt, and after Egypt was totally whipped, he lead the people from out of Egypt to the Promised Land. Now, remember that Egypt is symbolic of the world. In the book of Revelation we see that the Israelites are scattered throughout the whole world and Jesus is going to return and with a mighty hand Jesus will rain plague after plague down on the whole world until it is essentially destroyed, and will then gather the descendants of Israel from around the whole world to the Promised Land, that is the land of Israel. That is what is going to happen. Moses' events point to the real gathering of the people found in Revelation. Almost all of the events in the Old Testament are only shadows of the events that will soon take place.

When I was first reading the Bible and trying to understand it I found the stories in the Old Testament very weird and strange. I mean, of all the ways that God could have delivered the Israelites out of Egypt he seemed to have picked a very strange one. What I mean is Moses, and the desert, and the Red Sea and such; very odd, very strange, very weird, but, as I began to understand how the Bible works I began to realize that those events were strange on purpose. God was showing shadows of what would happen much later.

Look at Moses and the Red Sea for example. That was pretty odd when you think of it. God could have simply wiped out the pursuing Egyptians and that would have been that, but he didn't. Instead he divides the waters and the people escape through the waters, while when the Egyptians try to pass through the waters they are killed. Well this is symbolic. I don't mean that it didn't happen just the way it is recorded; no it did happen that way, but the meaning must be discerned. The water represents baptism which is symbolic of death and rebirth. So, Moses took the children out of the world and they died to the world and were reborn to live a new life for God. That is symbolically what happened. To show this important information the events played out the way that they did.

> **1 Corinthians 10:1–2**
> **For I do not want you to be ignorant of the fact, brothers, that our forefathers were all under the cloud and that they all passed through the sea. ² They were all baptized into Moses in the cloud and in the sea.** (NIV84)
>
> **Romans 6:3**
> **Or don't you know that all of us who were baptized into Christ Jesus were baptized into his death?** (NIV84)

Baptism is itself symbolic and the whole Red Sea episode was a shadow

of Jesus' baptism.

All of these things that happened in Egypt point to Christ Jesus and the reality that he brought. We find ourselves in the world, and God is in Christ leading us out of the world, through death, to life eternal. We can die to the world and be born-again in Christ, so that we can live for God and with God in heaven.

The shadows are not the things themselves. It is important to understand this. The events in the Old Testament are not the fulfillment of God's promises but only glimpses of the coming salvation.

We, as we go through the biblical scenario, will see many of these shadows and we will also see in the prophecies the actual real events.

The Players
Chapter Fifteen

*I*N THIS SECTION WE WILL be examining the different major beings or person-types that are revealed in the biblical story. I have
called them the players out of no disrespect. I only mean that
within God's plan there are beings of different types that are doing different things for different reasons. In this section I am just pointing out some of these types and the reasons for what they do. There are
three major categories of players: Divine being(s), spirit beings, physical world beings.

Spirit Beings

*M*OST EVERYONE KNOWS THAT GOD and the angels are spirit
beings, but what does that mean? Did you know that the word
spirit and the word ghost mean the same thing? The New International
Version of the Holy Bible uses the word spirit while the King James
Authorized Version uses the word ghost. We tend to think of a ghost as
being the whispery leftover of a real person. It is commonly thought
that when a person dies that some essence of the person lives on in
some ineffectual vaporous form that really has nothing to do nor can
really do anything.

I have mentioned before that heaven is far more real than the physical universe because heaven exists forever and the physical universe is
only a temporary place. Knowing this we can know that the spirit is not

some whispery vapor of nothingness, but rather is the more real, that is, the eternal person that animates the temporary animal body. The spirit person within you dominates your whole being. The spirit being within you is your soul. This being the case we can understand that spirits, or ghosts, are not insubstantial beings. The thing about spirit beings is that they are not subject to natural laws and so they can appear and disappear at will, giving the impression that they are insubstantial.

John 4:24
God is spirit, and his worshipers must worship in spirit and in truth." (NIV84)

There is nothing more real than God; therefore, spirit is more real than physical. Just because you can't see spirit with your physical world eyes doesn't mean that this is not so. The physical universe is unable to touch the spirit, but the spirit can touch both spirit and physical.

Spirit is undetectable with physical universe instrumentation. But, man is not just a physical world being, he is a spirit world being too. Man can detect the spirit universe, but only on a very subtle level.

Job 7:11
"Therefore I will not keep silent; I will speak out in the anguish of my spirit, I will complain in the bitterness of my soul. (NIV84)

Isaiah 26:9
My soul yearns for you in the night; in the morning my spirit longs for you. When your judgments come upon the earth, the people of the world learn righteousness. (NIV84)

Both of these passages from the Old Testament show us that there is a very close connection between the spirit and the soul. We see here the two words used in the same sentence to show the connection between them—soul and spirit.

1 Thessalonians 5:23
May God himself, the God of peace, sanctify you through and through. May your whole spirit, soul and body be kept blameless at the coming of our Lord Jesus Christ. (NIV84)

Hebrews 4:12
For the word of God is living and active. Sharper than any double-edged sword, it penetrates even to dividing soul and spirit, joints and marrow; it judges the thoughts and attitudes of the heart. (NIV84)

Here we see a little fine tuning on the topic of the spirit and the soul.

Your soul is you, the real you, the eternal you; your body is not. The person inside that makes you, you; is your soul. You, that is, your soul, is a spirit-person, and not at all a physical universe person. The spirit-person you is currently living within a physical world body so that you can experience the physical universe. This is God's will for you at this time.

If God were to remove the spirit person from within your body, what would be left would be a soulless animal; a more intelligent ape. You might be the smartest ape, but an ape nonetheless. It is the spirit person within, your soul, that makes you a human being, a being created in the image and likeness of God.

We can think of spirit in a way that is similar to the way we think of energy and atoms and such. Heaven is spirit while the universe is energy/matter; two totally dissimilar realities, or using modern pseudo-scientific jargon we would say that heaven and the physical universe are alternate universes, but in reality heaven is real and the physical is only temporary.

God

IT IS VERY CLEAR THAT God is a spirit.

John 4:24
God is spirit, and his worshipers must worship in spirit and in truth." (NIV84)

The Lord God being spirit means that he is not a physical universe being, that is, he is not made out of energy/matter. If God were made out of energy then he would be subject to time, which he is not.

It is very important to understand that the spirit world is not some vague, not as real, world. It is more real than the physical universe, because it was from the spirit that the physical was made, and when the physical is no more, the spirit will still be. The spirit is eternal, and the physical is temporary. We don't actually know anything about the makeup of spirit. God did not explain spirit to us in this way. We simply know that God is spirit and that we too have a spirit person within us. One thing that man has discovered is that we cannot, with our physical world instruments, detect even the existence of anything spirit. We would have a much easier time detecting light with a microphone than detecting spirit with any physical world instrumentation.

The Trinity

MAN HAS TWO NATURES. HE is both spirit and he is physical. God is spirit, but he has also manifested himself in the physical universe through the person of Jesus Christ and also we see that God's spirit is invisibly at work in the earth, so what we have are three mani-festations of God Almighty, commonly called the trinity.

The Father

GOD HAS MANY NAMES IN the Bible and each of them is important to understand. They each say something about his nature. There can be nothing more important in this world than knowing God.

The name that is most important to us is the one that Jesus gave us and that is the name Father. God may be all-powerful (he is), and he may be all-knowing (he is) and he may be the creator of heaven and earth (again, he is) but the name that is most important to us is Father because that name relates to us in a very personal way. The name Father tells us of a relationship that exists between God and man, or I should say, a relationship that can exist.

What I am saying is this: God's limitless attributes are there, and they are at work, but how do they really help us. What I mean is, if God is an all-powerful and all-knowing person but doesn't care about me, then how does knowing his all-powerful attributes help me? How would such a God be anything personal to me? There is no way that I can reach his level of perfection. Before him I stand condemned no matter how hard I try to rise to his level. I can never, ever, stand on God's level in anything. So, knowledge of God's attributes doesn't really help me very much if all they do is point to my destruction, but the name Father tells a differ-ent possibility. I can be a family member. I can be loved by virtue of my relationship to him. Now, that means something.

When we think of the Trinity, however, we usually think of God the Father as being the all-powerful God who sits on the throne in heaven and judges the peoples of the earth. He is the All Mighty. He may be the Father (he is) but he is also the All Mighty God. So, considering my total incompetence as a son of God his father status is a little more scary than totally helpful.

The Son

HE ALL MIGHTY GOD CREATED man for a reason. He wants to be our personal Father. He wants to have a loving relationship with us and for us to have a personal and loving relationship with him. In order to do this it was/is necessary that he reveal himself to us in a way that we can see and know him. You cannot love what you do not know. Jesus Christ is the perfect revelation of God himself in a form that we can see and understand.

Jesus represents (and is) the perfect human relationship with the Father. If a person wanted to be a perfectly pleasing person to God Almighty he or she need only be exactly like Jesus. We have a role model in Christ Jesus.

Jesus is much more than a role model, but he is nonetheless a perfect role model. Jesus is an exact representation of God Almighty but he is also the Savior. God Almighty is our Savior also because God is/was in Christ Jesus and Jesus is/was in God. But, as we saw earlier in this book, we are in God Almighty and God Almighty is in us.

Jesus is as much God as can be, but he is also as much a man as can be.

Hebrews 2:10–18
In bringing many sons to glory, it was fitting that God, for whom and through whom everything exists, should make the author of their salvation perfect through suffering. [11] Both the one who makes men holy and those who are made holy are of the same family. So Jesus is not ashamed to call them brothers. [12] He says,
"I will declare your name to my brothers; in the presence of the congregation I will sing your praises."
[13] And again, "I will put my trust in him."
And again he says, "Here am I, and the children God has given me."
[14] Since the children have flesh and blood, he too shared in their humanity so that by his death he might destroy him who holds the power of death—that is, the devil— [15] and free those who all their lives were held in slavery by their fear of death. [16] For surely it is not angels he helps, but Abraham's descendants. [17] For this reason he had to be made like his brothers in every way, in order that he might become a merciful and faithful high priest in service to God, and that he might make atonement for the sins of the people. [18] Because he himself suffered when he was tempted, he is able to help those who are being tempted.
(NIV84)

Colossians 1:15
He is the image of the invisible God, the firstborn over all creation. (NIV84)

Hebrews 1:1–3
In the past God spoke to our forefathers through the prophets at many times and in various ways, ² but in these last days he has spoken to us by his Son, whom he appointed heir of all things, and through whom he made the universe. ³ The Son is the radiance of God's glory and the exact representation of his being, sustaining all things by his powerful word... (NIV84)

Also see: Acts 3:15; 2 Corinthians 4:4; Romans 9:5; Colossians 2:9; Isaiah 9:6-7 and more.

We can say that if God Almighty became a human being, so that we could see and know him, he would be Jesus Christ. This point is made perfectly clear in the Scriptures. Anyone that would tell you different does not belong to God and the Scriptures call that person an antichrist.

The Holy Spirit

THE FATHER IS IN HEAVEN and Jesus was a flesh and blood man, but the power of God is always at work in the physical universe. God's presence at work in the universe is through what he calls the Holy Spirit. The Holy Spirit is not a Casper-like ghost that goes from place to place, but rather God's Spirit is everywhere within the physical universe.

A spirit in this world is more or less invisible. We cannot see any spirits unless they make themselves visible to us. We cannot even detect our own spirit natures, no matter how hard we try.

My understanding of the Trinity is not that God is broken up into three parts, but rather God is most definitely One and he explains himself in this three-person way. This Trinity explanation is much like the explanation of ourselves. We have a body, which has a physical organ, the brain, which animates our body and have a mind, but we are not our bodies and neither are we our minds, but rather there is a spirit person, that is somehow in there someplace, and that spirit person is the real us. If someone were to kill my body that doesn't mean that they have killed me.

Luke 12:4–5
"I tell you, my friends, do not be afraid of those who kill the body and after that can do no more. ⁵ But I will show you

whom you should fear: Fear him who, after the killing of the body, has power to throw you into hell. Yes, I tell you, fear him. (Jesus Christ) (NIV84)

My point here is not that you are two people, but rather you have two natures. One is permanent and the other is temporary, but two nonetheless. God too is a single spirit person that we call the Father, but he has made a human body for himself so that he could be experienced firsthand by people, and he also maintains the very fabric of the physical universe by his person and this is done in a sort of invisible way. All of this was done for your benefit, so that you can understand that the Creator of the universe is not some non-personal happenstance of an energy form, but rather a person himself. God is a person, and he is knowable. God has made himself knowable through Jesus Christ and through the Bible. The person of God can be known. The person of the Holy Spirit is a little harder to explain, but I will give you an analogy. Imagine that we live in God Almighty and that we are sustained by his invisible blood which represents the Holy Spirit. We would not call this invisible blood God Almighty because it is only his blood. This invisible life sustaining blood is however part of God and cannot be separated from God any more than your blood can be separated from you. You are not your blood, but your blood is necessary for the sustainment of your body. The Holy Spirit can be sort of thought of like this, only far far more. For those people that are not Christians the Holy Spirit is very much like I have explained, but for those that have a faith-bond with God through Jesus Christ, the Holy Spirit forms a much more robust link between yourself and God the Father. When a person opens themselves up to God, without limit God establishes a personal communication link between them and himself. Imagine, if you will, that we are a single computer and God is a mega-computer and when we are bonded to God with a faith-bond we are sort of made part of God's network. We become a sort of node on the God Internet. In this way the Holy Spirit becomes a sort of IP protocol that allows us to communicate with each other directly, that is, between God and us. Now further imagine that if you are not connected to the God network, then you must receive your information from God in smoke signals, OR and this is a big or, you can receive information about God from a book, which is really how it works until your spiritual Ethernet cable is connected to God. The Bible is our information source concerning God until the network link is established. We still need the Bible even after our network connection is made, because God is going to speak to

you in Bible. You must learn Bible. If you don't know Bible very well then you will receive information on the network but it will be hard for you to decipher.

I hope that you understand that I am using very limited words here to explain these things. God is not a computer and we are not computers connected on a network. I am only trying to explain the relationships that exist between us and God. I am using these worldly images so that you might gain some understanding. Please don't make too much of my computer analogy.

> **Romans 8:9**
> **You, however, are controlled not by the sinful nature but by the Spirit, if the Spirit of God lives in you. And if anyone does not have the Spirit of Christ, he does not belong to Christ.** (NIV84)

We see in this passage that another name of the Holy Spirit is the Spirit of Christ. The Holy Spirit and the Spirit of Christ are one and the same.

The Father, the Son, and the Holy Spirit are all one and the same person. They are manifestations of the same person. You cannot say that one does anything apart from the others.

God's Nature

> **Jeremiah 9:23–24**
> **This is what the Lord says: "Let not the wise man boast of his wisdom or the strong man boast of his strength or the rich man boast of his riches, ²⁴ but let him who boasts boast about this: that he understands and knows me, that I am the Lord, who exercises kindness, justice and righteousness on earth, for in these I delight," declares the Lord.** (NIV84)

O YOU KNOW GOD IN this way? Do you think of God as a person (being) that is identified by his kindness?

> **Galatians 5:22–23**
> **But the fruit of the Spirit is love, joy, peace, patience, kindness, goodness, faithfulness, ²³ gentleness and self-control.** (NIV84)

This passage says that if you belong to God then this fruit will grow in you. Fruit grows from the plant that it grows from. Jesus said…

> **Matthew 7:15–20**
> **"Watch out for false prophets. They come to you in sheep's**

clothing, but inwardly they are ferocious wolves. [16] By their fruit you will recognize them. Do people pick grapes from thornbushes, or figs from thistles? [17] Likewise every good tree bears good fruit, but a bad tree bears bad fruit. [18] A good tree cannot bear bad fruit, and a bad tree cannot bear good fruit. [19] Every tree that does not bear good fruit is cut down and thrown into the fire. [20] Thus, by their fruit you will recognize them. (NIV84)

If you think that you know the Lord God Almighty then you should know that in the core of your being he is the perfect expression of the qualities that are expressed in Galatians 5:22-23. I say in the core of your being and not in your mind. People frequently (almost always) acknowledge things in their mind as being true, but deep down inside they don't really believe it. When you know that God is good, then you are a changed man or a changed woman. Satan doesn't know this. Satan doesn't know that God is good. Satan sees God as hard and powerful. To see God as he is, requires that you seek him with all of your heart and that you become like him in your heart. It is through your becoming like him that you really come to know him. Even if you only become like him in little flashes, in which case your understanding will come in little flashes too. Learning about God can be a little discouraging. We try to be good but our real selves keep popping up and shoving ourselves in our own faces, but try not to get discouraged. Little flashes of obedience, and the resulting little flashes of insight, are more than those that the world gets. If you get enough little flashes you will know God intimately.

As much as you can, imitate God and his goodness. Keep coming back to that. Don't give up in self-disgust. Do as many little acts of goodness that you can and in time you will grow. As you keep coming back and doing these selfless acts of love, you will in itsy bitsy bits, become more and more like God, that is, you will become the person that you imitate. Don't forget that God is an active participant in all of this. God is actively working in each and every aspect of your life. Don't forget this; rely on it.

The Vine

ONE OF THE SYMBOLS OF God is that of a vine, or rather the root of the vine. The root of a plant supplies the water and nutrients to the rest of the plant.

John 15:1–6
"I am the true vine, and my Father is the gardener. [2] He

cuts off every branch in me that bears no fruit, while every branch that does bear fruit he prunes so that it will be even more fruitful. [3] You are already clean because of the word I have spoken to you. [4] Remain in me, and I will remain in you. No branch can bear fruit by itself; it must remain in the vine. Neither can you bear fruit unless you remain in me. [5] "I am the vine; you are the branches. If a man remains in me and I in him, he will bear much fruit; apart from me you can do nothing. [6] If anyone does not remain in me, he is like a branch that is thrown away and withers; such branches are picked up, thrown into the fire and burned. (NIV84)

This is a very important concept to understand. One must remain in God to bear godly fruit. Notice that Jesus tells you to remain in him. This is an active thing to do. One doesn't just confess Jesus as their personal Lord and Savior and then all is fine and done. Jesus tells you to remain in him. You have something to do. You must remain in him.

The man and the woman in the Garden of Eden listened to the Devil and thought that what the Devil said made good sense. They wanted to be like God and so they disobeyed God and followed their own path to wisdom and knowledge. This clearly turned out to be a disaster, as all godless plans turn out. We must remain firmly in him and with him. God is the Father and we are the children. As we remain in him, day after day, year after year, God's nutrients enable us to grow into mature children of God.

Romans 11:16–24
If the part of the dough offered as firstfruits is holy, then the whole batch is holy; if the root is holy, so are the branches. [17] If some of the branches have been broken off, and you, though a wild olive shoot, have been grafted in among the others and now share in the nourishing sap from the olive root, [18] do not boast over those branches. If you do, consider this: You do not support the root, but the root supports you. [19] You will say then, "Branches were broken off so that I could be grafted in." [20] Granted. But they were broken off because of unbelief, and you stand by faith. Do not be arrogant, but be afraid. [21] For if God did not spare the natural branches, he will not spare you either.
[22] Consider therefore the kindness and sternness of God: sternness to those who fell, but kindness to you, provided that you continue in his kindness. Otherwise, you also will be cut off. [23] And if they do not persist in unbelief, they will be grafted in, for God is able to graft them in again. [24] After all, if you were cut out of an olive tree that is wild by na-

ture, and contrary to nature were grafted into a cultivated olive tree, how much more readily will these, the natural branches, be grafted into their own olive tree! (NIV84)

The understanding of this passage is very important if you want to understand the prophecies. Here we see the analogy of the vine/root and the branches, but with a little twist. We see that the Jews (Israelites) are the true branches of the vine, and we Gentiles are wild branches that have unnaturally been grafted into the vine. We see also, and this is very important, that the Jews are still loved by God and are considered holy by him. It is a very big mistake to think that we Gentile believers are somehow better than the Jews.

A few more sentences down the chapter we are clearly told that the Jews will be restored to God.

Another thing to notice in this passage is that we are told to remain in him again, that is, to maintain our faith relationship with him, or we will be cut off like the Jews were cut off. A relationship with God is an active thing. God is always faithful, but we must take great care that we do not get side-tracked and start perusing earthly paths.

To sum this up a bit, we must understand that God is the source of everything, and that we Gentile believers have been temporally grafted into God's covenant, and that we enter into this relationship by faith and maintain it by that same faith. Those that get side-tracked and no longer produce the fruit of the Spirit will be pruned off to wither and die, but those that continue to produce fruit for the kingdom of God will remain. When the time is right, after the last Gentile believer has entered into the kingdom with Christ, then the whole community of Jews will be brought back into the covenant with God.

Take care that pride does not prevent you from seeing this. This truth is clearly there in Romans to see.

Angels

E HAVE SEEN THAT GOD is a spirit being, and that Jesus has God's spirit person within him, as does the Holy Spirit which is just another name for God's soul. Angels are another type of spirit being that the Bible tells us about. Angels are to God, as cats are to dogs, or horses are to elephants. Both God and the angels are spirit beings, and not at all animal beings, and cats, dogs, horses and elephants are physical world beings, but not spirit beings. I am using the word be-

ings a little loosely here. Animals are living beings, but are not eternal persons, as it were.

The angels are spirit beings, or if you like, spirit persons of a slightly different kind than God and were created by God, that is, they do not reproduce. They were created holy, that is, they have faith relationships with God Almighty.

People do not become angels and angels can never become people. There are angels and there are human people.

The angels are subject to God, that is, they submit to God like we are told to do so ourselves. I am talking about God's holy angels here. It is evident that a full third of the angels listened to Satan and broke faith with God as Satan did. We will call these angels, the fallen angels. The Bible calls them Satan's angels.

We know from the Bible that the angels are spirit beings that are eternal. We also know that they are neither male nor female. They do not propagate.

Matthew 22:29–30
Jesus replied, "You are in error because you do not know the Scriptures or the power of God. [30] At the resurrection people will neither marry nor be given in marriage; they will be like the angels in heaven. (NIV84)

In the Bible we see angels represented in a male form. This does not mean that they are males. Angels do not have an actual sex, any more than God does. Each and every spirit being in the Bible is depicted as a male. And humankind, if symbolized in an image, is always depicted as a female. This male and female depiction is not to be understood literally but shows us the relationships that exist between spirit beings and natural world beings. Please understand that none of the angels are actually males and neither is God actually a male. Male and female are really only physical world differences that exist for propagation reasons only. I will talk more about this later.

The fact that angels are spirit beings is known because they are eternal. The same angels that were there long ago are here today. If they were physical world beings then they would age and eventually die. Nothing in the natural world can exist forever.

HE TWENTY-EIGHTH CHAPTER OF THE book of Ezekiel gives us some very interesting information concerning the angel Satan the Devil. Did you know that Satan was an angel? This passage in-

forms us that he had been anointed as a guardian cherub. I don't know the hierarchy of the angels, but a guardian cherub must be up there with the highest. In the Holy of Holies, the most sacred part of God's Tabernacle, rested the Arc of the Covenant, and placed on the cover of the Arc were statues of two guardian cherubs. I have heard it said that they guarded God's holiness, which I don't know if that is true, but I do know that being there, over the Ark of the Covenant, was an important place to be. So, from Ezekiel 28 we can see that Satan was a very important angel.

In the first part of this chapter we see that the narrative is directed to the prince of Tyre, who is clearly a man, but then in verse eleven we see that the narrative switches to the king of Tyre who is an angel and not a man, and it is evident that it is talking about the fallen angel, Satan.

Ezekiel 28:11–15
The word of the Lord came to me: [12] **"Son of man, take up a lament concerning the king of Tyre and say to him: 'This is what the Sovereign Lord says: " 'You were the model of perfection, full of wisdom and perfect in beauty.** [13] **You were in Eden, the garden of God; every precious stone adorned you: ruby, topaz and emerald, chrysolite, onyx and jasper, sapphire, turquoise and beryl. Your settings and mountings were made of gold; on the day you were created they were prepared.** [14] **You were anointed as a guardian cherub, for so I ordained you. You were on the holy mount of God; you walked among the fiery stones.** [15] **You were blameless in your ways from the day you were created till wickedness was found in you.** (NIV84)

Notice that the king of Tyre was an anointed guardian cherub and that he had been created. Men are born and apart from Adam and Eve none are said to be created.

We can understand that this 'king' is the power behind the prince, that is, Satan is the spiritual power behind the human ruler of the nation of Tyre. This is a very important understanding to make. We humans tend to think that we are masters of our own destiny but this is nothing but pride talking. We will be exploring the dynamics of earth rule, and destiny, later in this book, for now please notice that this guardian cherub was the 'king' over the 'prince'.

Notice too, very carefully, what this passage says about Satan. He was the '**model of perfection, full of wisdom and perfect in beauty**' when he was created. Wow, what a statement. We are not really told exactly what Satan's position in heaven was relative to the other angels, but it

is clear that he was one of the most important, if important is a word of relevance here. From reading the Bible we can see that God organizes authority in a hierarchal structure, that is, God being on top and seated on his right is Jesus and we do not know who is seated to his left but are told that someone will be. It is evident that there are those that are just under Jesus in authority and then others under them, and so on, and so on.

We can see from reading passages about angels that they are not all the same. Some are more powerful, capable, and wise than others. Satan was evidently a powerful angel and by looking at what occurred we can deduce that he was probably pretty high up in the heavenly hierarchy. I say this because in the Scriptures we see that a third of all the angels put their faith in Satan over God and for this to happen he must have been some angel.

We can also see from this passage that Satan was a very special being, until **'wickedness was found' in** him. Satan was so special, and so beautiful, and so full of wisdom, that he became filled with pride, which spiritually speaking is the kiss of death. The Bible warns us against pride probably more than against anything else. Pride is the giant killer. Pride is the poison that can kill the highest and the greatest. Satan looked at his own beauty and wisdom and he was filled with pride and he said…'[12] **How you have fallen from heaven, O morning star, son of the dawn! You have been cast down to the earth, you who once laid low the nations!** [13] **You said in your heart, "I will ascend to heaven; I will raise my throne above the stars of God; I will sit enthroned on the mount of assembly, on the utmost heights of the sacred mountain.** [14] **I will ascend above the tops of the clouds; I will make myself like the Most High."' Isaiah 14:12–14** (NIV84)

If a being loses track of the spiritual force of love within them, and then puts themselves above their station, (the station that God ordained for them), they then have broken faith with God. If you have faith in God, then you know that whatever God does or says is perfect, and so if you put your faith in anything other than the Word of God then you have broken the faith-bond that you once had with God. A person can't have it both ways. A person can't have their faith in God and in themselves at the same time. Either God is the supreme authority or he is not. Pride is so dangerous because to have pride means you have taken your focus off love and have put it on yourself. We are all working toward the good of all and to do that you must be operating with God. Love sustains existence. God sustains existence. God is love.

Let me give you an example: Within a human family the husband serves the needs of his wife and children and the wife also serves the needs of her husband and children. If either the husband or the wife put themselves above the needs of the family, the family will suffer. It is the duty of the parents to serve their family. This is a sacred and holy duty. All existence is just exactly like that. God serves the needs of his whole family, as it were. He never puts himself above others. He is above others because that is what is right and best for all. Do you see the subtle distinction here? God is above all because he is, not because he wants to be. He is above all by virtue of his being Love.

Each and every one of us must accept the position that we are in. We must strive to be more perfect in love for loves own sake. As we submit to love, and love guides and reveals itself to us, then God, the ultimate love, will move us to the place where we should be. If we look at ourselves and then are motivated to move ourselves to any other place then we are no longer in love.

Because God IS love, and ONLY God is love, God must be the one that all others take direction from. To take direction from anything other than love would be harmful to existence. Now, I ask you, what should be the guiding light for all, that is, for each and every one of us? Anything other than love will eat itself to death. Only love can sustain forever and ever. And this being so means that God, who is the person of Divine Love, must be the source. To reject God as the Source is to place yourself above him and by extension, above other people; this is societal cancer. To recognize God as love and to submit to love because love is love is the beginning of true wisdom.

Now, my point in saying all of this is to show just what the angel Satan did and why it was so bad. All angels know so much more than we do about spiritual matters. None of us can compare ourselves with Satan, or any of the angels for that matter. It is not difficult to see why Satan thought so highly of himself, and where that took him. It is not too difficult to see also why other angels thought along similar lines. Being a person makes one think that one's self is more important than the all. Let us look a little more at Satan and what happened.

Satan was a very powerful and beautiful angel and he saw himself as his own person, so he said in his heart, I don't need anyone over me, I am my own man, I can determine my own destiny.

Ezekiel 28:16–19
**Through your widespread trade you were filled with vio-
lence, and you sinned. So I drove you in disgrace from the
mount of God, and I expelled you, O guardian cherub,
from among the fiery stones. ¹⁷ Your heart became proud
on account of your beauty, and you corrupted your wisdom
because of your splendor. So I threw you to the earth; I
made a spectacle of you before kings. ¹⁸ By your many sins
and dishonest trade you have desecrated your sanctuaries.
So I made a fire come out from you, and it consumed you,
and I reduced you to ashes on the ground in the sight of all
who were watching. ¹⁹ All the nations who knew you are
appalled at you; you have come to a horrible end and will
be no more.' " (NIV84)**

In this continuation of what we just read in Ezekiel. We can see some
more very valuable information concerning Satan's downfall and from
this we can see potential pitfalls for ourselves. The above passage says
that his fall was because of his beauty. Now that is interesting. Satan
was so spiritually lovely that he came to believe in himself. He separated himself from God, that is, he broke faith with God and became
his own man, because he came to believe in himself. Now, what I find
really interesting in this is that Satan was never created in the image and
likeness of God, as we were. Man's spiritual beauty must be awesome
indeed. What I mean to say, is that man was created in the very image
and likeness of God Almighty and this must make us far more beautiful
and capable than Satan ever was, (on the inside). Now, this being true,
and if Satan couldn't handle his beauty and wisdom, how much more
would man not be able to handle his? You must really think about what
I am saying here. It is very important.

This explains so much. This explains why God created the physical
universe in the first place, and placed us, his actual children, created in
his image and after his likeness, into animal bodies that are always one
breath away from death. Inside we are wondrous, outside we are smelly
powerless animals. This was to keep us humble; to keep us from pride.
God kept our true natures hidden from us, and made the physical so seemingly dominant, to help us stay away from the same pit Satan fell into.

God did make us king of the animals, so to say, to fuel our pride if
we were so inclined, but for a man to place himself above God is pretty
ridiculous; prideful man denies God's existence in order to elevate himself
to the top of the food chain, so to say.

Looking back to Ezekiel, and what it has to say about Satan, we must understand the nature of how the prophecies are written. Remember that God is in eternity and we are in time. The prophecies are, for the most part, looking at things from the eternal perspective. God says that he cast Satan down to the earth and then destroyed him there, but this has not yet happened in our time frame. God speaks as though it is a done deal, and it is, but from our perspective it hasn't happened yet. This brings us to a very important point and that is that nothing that God says can or will ever fail. I have mentioned this before, about how Jesus said that not one comma or period in the Bible will fail to happen before the end, and that heaven and earth would pass away before any of the Bible does.

God's plan cannot fail. The question is not, whether or not any part of the Bible will fail, but rather will you be on board with God, or not; more on this later.

Another interesting aspect of Ezekiel 28 as it relates to Satan, and to his destruction; the Bible says that God threw him down and made a spectacle of him, and his downfall, before kings. This brings us to another very important thing to understand. The whole plan of God is being recorded, so to say, and will be watchable to every spiritual being in heaven. It chronicles the effect of sin, not just to and for man, but also to and for the angels as well. What I mean is that before any of this occurred the angels didn't understand sin and death. No one had ever sinned and died before. Now, after the fact, we can all look at the history of sin and death and decide if it is good for us or bad for us. That is really the purpose of the Bible. Do you really want to go the way of sin and death, or would you rather hookup with God and believe in him and in his way of love, faith and hope? Remember we have not yet reached the end of the plan, but we can look into the prophecies and see the end by faith too. We can see what has not yet happened, and know that it most surely will happen, and so we can see the whole story and then decide what we want. This is why I am writing this book. I want to explain how things work, and show you the whole plan of God before it happens, so that you can decide what to do about it, now while you are still living in the flesh. My purpose in this is God's purpose too. This is why God put all of this information into the Bible in the first place.

Symbolized

HE LORD GOD ALMIGHTY IS symbolically represented by the Sun. The sun is, after all, the source of all life on the earth. We use the light from the sun to see what we are doing and without it we would be in virtual darkness and without the sun we would soon die.

Jesus is symbolically represented by the moon. It is an interesting, and I am sure, not accidental, fact, that the moon when viewed from the earth is the same size as the sun. When we look at Jesus we see God the father with his glory turned down low, so that we can see him without burning out our eyes.

> **Genesis 1:16**
> **God made two great lights—the greater light to govern the day and the lesser light to govern the night. He also made the stars.** (NIV84)

This passage is literal as most are, but it is also symbolic, also as most passages are. Notice the interesting word govern.

The Sun and to Moon symbolically represent God and his revealed truth. In the day we live in God's presence. At night we cannot see God, which is symbolic of our world after the fall of man. After the fall we lost our connection to the Lord God and so we mostly walk in darkness. The Bible is a source of light in this dark world. When we read the Bible we can see the light of God Almighty. Jesus was a manifestation of God's truth in the world in human form. When we look at Jesus we see a picture of God Almighty with his glory turned down low.

> **Psalm 89:35–37**
> **Once for all, I have sworn by my holiness— and I will not lie to David— 36 that his line will continue forever and his throne endure before me like the sun; 37 it will be established forever like the moon, the faithful witness in the sky."** (NIV84)

Notice that the moon is a faithful witness in the sky. Faithful means that it is accurate and is therefore an accurate witness of God, which is displayed in the sky.

The last celestial objects that we can see in the sky are the stars. The stars represent God's created angels.

> **Revelation 12:3-4**
> **Then another sign appeared in heaven: an enormous red dragon with seven heads and ten horns and seven crowns**

on his heads. ⁴ His tail swept a third of the stars out of the sky and flung them to the earth. (NIV84)

We see here Satan depicted here as a red dragon and his tail swept a third of the stars from the sky and flung them to the earth. This is clearly symbolic language. We see an explanation for this which quickly follows the above passage in Revelation.

Revelation 12:9
The great dragon was hurled down—that ancient serpent called the devil, or Satan, who leads the whole world astray. He was hurled to the earth, and his angels with him. (NIV84)

So clearly the dragon is identified for us as Satan and the stars must be his angels, that is, it is evident here that a third of all the angels listened to Satan, and those angels thought as the woman in the garden did, that they too wanted to be like God, knowing good and evil. They must have also thought that it was a good thing to gain this knowledge and so they took it upon themselves to gain this knowledge by themselves. They elevated themselves and so they fell.

Do you see how this symbolic language of the celestial objects is being used? I find this all very interesting. There is much more information to be gleaned in these passages but for now this is enough. Later we will look into the seven heads and the crowns and horns.

I find it very interesting that a whole third of the angels fell away from God. This fact tells us first off that the angels can fall away. After knowing what I know now about the Bible and the angels I find this a remarkable fact. Given the outcome for the fallen angels we can only assume that they did not understand the full ramifications of their act of rebellion. This was also the situation in the Garden of Eden when the Serpent seduced the woman into rebellion. In the Garden, before the fall, man did not understand the full ramifications of an act of willful disobedience. Now, for anyone that can read a Bible in faith, the ramifications are very evident and very grim, to say the least. Again, this information regarding the effect or result of willful disobedience is one of the main purposes of the Bible. Without the Bible you would have no way in the world of understanding this-none whatsoever. With the Bible we can see and understand a lot of things. Oh, I thank God for the Bible!

It is evident that the angels, like man, both have the free will to obey God or not.

One last thing that the symbolism makes known to us is the fact that

if the Sun represents God the Father, then living in his presence makes everything very visible. But because we live in a fallen world we live in the Night (symbolically) and so when the Moon is out we can see reasonably well, but on a moonless night visibility is very poor. All of the angels combined, including Satan, can't illuminate things hardly at all. I have heard people suggest that Jesus Christ and Satan are more or less equals. They say that one is good and the other is bad. The fallacy of this thinking is easily seen in this symbolism. Jesus puts out, I don't know, maybe a thousand times more light than all of the angels combined. Satan is only one star. You can't really compare Jesus with Satan. It is total foolishness to do so.

Man

E HAVE LOOKED BRIEFLY AT the spirit beings that exist and so now we will look at the beings or creatures of the earth. On the planet we have a myriad of various animal types. You and I both know, without any doubts, that there are animals ranging from microscopic to much bigger than us. I hope that you also understand that your body is nothing but an animal body. It is nothing, only an animal body, and nothing less. You are not your body. I know that I am repeating this, but it is okay to go over things more than once. I frequently read and reread books, and each time I reread something I see more than I did before.

There is something about the natural world that you really need to keep in the forefront of your mind, and that is the fact, that the natural world, in fact the whole natural universe, in all its enormity and glory, is only temporary. (I hope that I have repeated that so many times now that you know it instantly.) This fact is clearly revealed in the Bible as we shall soon see, but it is also known to our physicists. The temporary nature of energy/ matter is known as entropy. Entropy says that eventually everything will grow cold and stop working. Now, granted, that this stopping of energy is a long long way away, but it nonetheless is coming and is unstoppable. The universe, however long lived, is temporary. It is not eternal.

The Bible tells us that Heaven is eternal. Heaven, therefore, cannot be made out of energy/matter, because anything made out of energy/matter must be temporary, because of entropy. This is not a critical thing to know but to me it is pretty interesting.

Hebrews 12:26–27
At that time his voice shook the earth, but now he has
promised, "Once more I will shake not only the earth but
also the heavens." ²⁷ The words "once more" indicate the
removing of what can be shaken—that is, created things—
so that what cannot be shaken may remain. (NIV84)

You have to read the symbolic words here to see what it is saying and to understand what I am saying concerning heaven and the physical universe. The Bible says that the heavens and the earth will be shaken, and that word shaken is explained here for us. This passage says that shaken means removed, and removed by a direct act of God. So what we see here is that in the same way that God spoke the universe into existence when he wanted it here, he will also remove it, when it suits him, probably also with spoken words. To receive the fact that the universe is temporary requires faith on your part, just as it is required concerning the creation of the physical universe. The Bible tells us that God spoke, and the universe came into existence, and that was that. Man has spent probably millions of man hours examining the universe and trying to determine where it came from, and can only see that it did come into existence from non-existence, but beyond that, science cannot tell you that God spoke it into existence. The Bible gives us this information. The Bible does not tell us how God did it. I am very certain that had the Bible told us how he did it, not one person on the earth would ever understand what was said. The power of creation from nothing is quite beyond us.

What I would like you to understand here is that our bodies are temporary too. I keep saying this because the world tells us dozens of times a day how important our bodies are. As a society we are obsessed with youth and health and longevity. Within the world the body is everything. From the world's perspective the body is everything. From the world's perspective when you grow old and die then you are gone-period. We are conceived and we grow, and are born, and then we develop, and eventually we grow old and die. That is the natural turn of events. Unless God intervenes that is what is going to happen. Oh, we might die sooner because of whatever reasons, but eventually, actually soon, we will all die. Our physical bodies are very temporary even if we live to be 1000 years old.

Job 34:14–15
If it were his intention and he withdrew his spirit and
breath, ¹⁵ all mankind would perish together and man
would return to the dust. (NIV84)

Ecclesiastes 3:20
**All go to the same place; all come from dust, and to dust all
return.** (NIV84)

Again we see symbolic words used to describe spiritual truths. Our
bodies come from the earth and to the earth they will return. We are
temporary. We are temporary, and we, that is, our bodies, are made from
temporary stuff.

However, and this is a gigantically big however, we are not our bodies.
Man is a hybrid. Do you understand what a hybrid is? It seems to be
all the rage today in automobile design. A hybrid automobile has both
an electric motor, and has an internal combustion engine. It can run on
some form of chemical power (gasoline or diesel, usually) or it can run
on electrical energy. Because it has two completely different forms of
operation it is said to be a hybrid.

Well man is a hybrid too. Man is the only hybrid being in heaven or
on earth. The angels are spirit and the animals are physical, but man has
an animal body, but inside is really an angel-like spirit. I say angel-like
loosely, actually we are more godlike than angel-like, but at this point that
would be picking nits. My point here is that man is really a godlike spirit
being that temporally lives inside an animal body. We are not animals that
have a spirit inside. To say that we are animals that have spirits inside
would be like saying that we are like automobiles with people inside
driving them—totally backwards. We are people that drive automobiles.

The fact that we are spirit being is so very important that almost everything else concerning our makeup is of no real important at all.

People that have no understanding look around at the world today and
mostly see themselves as human beings, that is, they see the physical
person as the only person. They can't see the spirit person, for the spirit
person cannot be seen with natural eyes, and so they think that the spirit
person does not exist. Medical science has tried to see the person inside
with all manner of instrumentation, but for the most part they have
failed. Medical science has determined that there is some invisible part
of a man that lives inside, they have determined that that part of a man
is the part that really drives the whole person, but they can't really find
that person. They call that inner person the subconscious mind. Medical
science cannot really understand what the subconscious mind is, because
the subconscious mind is not really of this creation. The subconscious
mind is the part of a person that is created in the image and likeness of

God himself, but this godlike spirit being has been hidden within—hardly detectable at all. The Bible tells us regarding this inner person…

Proverbs 4:23
Above all else, guard your heart, for it is the wellspring of life. (NIV84)

The wellspring of life; the source of your true life. The heart is just another name for your inner person, that is, the spirit being you. This passage says that above all else guard your inner person. I imagine that the psychiatrists of the world, who are operating in the dark, because they don't really understand the fundamentals of human make up, would agree with this proverb. Our subconscious mind, the real you, is a sensitive and delicate being. This godlike spirit person is you, but exists just below your direct awareness level, and is living in this corrupted world being affected by everything that it sees and hears. Evil, that is, anti-love motivations, are constantly bombarding your inner person. You must resist the self-directed desires and selfish motivations of the flesh, which war against your inner person. As I said before you are a hybrid being; you have two natures, both of which have desires, but only one of your natures is eternal, only one is ultimately important, only one is you; the person that does not die.

Romans 7:14–25
We know that the law is spiritual; but I am unspiritual, sold as a slave to sin. [15] I do not understand what I do. For what I want to do I do not do, but what I hate I do. [16] And if I do what I do not want to do, I agree that the law is good. [17] As it is, it is no longer I myself who do it, but it is sin living in me. [18] I know that nothing good lives in me, that is, in my sinful nature. For I have the desire to do what is good, but I cannot carry it out. [19] For what I do is not the good I want to do; no, the evil I do not want to do—this I keep on doing. [20] Now if I do what I do not want to do, it is no longer I who do it, but it is sin living in me that does it. 21 So I find this law at work: When I want to do good, evil is right there with me. [22] For in my inner being I delight in God's law; [23] but I see another law at work in the members of my body, waging war against the law of my mind and making me a prisoner of the law of sin at work within my members. [24] What a wretched man I am! Who will rescue me from this body of death? [25] Thanks be to God—through Jesus Christ our Lord! So then, I myself in my mind am a slave to God's law, but in the sinful nature a slave to the law of sin. (NIV84)

The dual nature of man is what this passage is talking about. Inside we are sensitive godlike spirit beings, but we live in crude self-centered animal bodies. Our bodies have drives that war against the love and joy and peace of the person inside. We are conflicted. We are two people; the animal person and the spirit person. Which will dominate? The inner spirit person can have a relationship with God, but the flesh cannot ever have anything to do with God. The inner person is the eternal you, the outer person is you too, but really only a result of yourself and of the world that has surrounded you.

Our human brains are where our minds reside. Our human brains are highly suggestible and programmable when they are developing. This is how the human mind develops. Your mind is greatly affected by everything that goes on around it, most especially during what we call your formative years. People know this. That is why they generally don't allow very young children to be exposed to certain environments. Well, the Scriptures tell us that our inner person is highly formative too. We must guard it with our life, literally. Our inner person is the person that will exist forever, and that makes it the only real important person you have. Your mind will die with the body, but the inner you, your subconscious person, your spirit being person, will live on—forever.

Most sensible adults protect their young children against exposure to negative activities for fear of contaminating them. The fact that they protect their children from evil shows that they do know what evil is, and that this evil should be avoided. The Scripture above warns you to guard your heart above all else, and is talking about you being smart enough to keep yourself away from those same evil things, even after you have become an adult. You too, even though you regard yourself as an adult, are highly susceptible to evil. Evil is seductive. Evil is a liar. Evil says, go on, it feels good, it won't hurt you, it's a thrill, but evil is a liar, evil wants to break you down so that it can dominate you, and your so-called friends that try to involve you in evil do not have divine love for you at heart.

Do you want to know what evil is? Evil is opposite of Divine Love. Suppose you had a God-Compass which, when you hold it, the needle points away from you, well an Evil-Compass would point towards you. I don't mean that you are the epitome of evil. What I do mean is that when your motivation is aimed toward yourself then beware, but when your motivation is for the benefit of others, then you are probably aimed

on the right path. An evil motive wants to elevate yourself, but to draw closer to the divine, is to allow yourself to be useful to God in the fulfillment of his motives. Another way of saying this is to say that you are willingly obedient to God. When you do not seek to elevate yourself, but rather, you seek to ignore yourself and do what God would have you do, then God, who sees all and knows all, will elevate you as he sees fit.

Divine love is the sustaining power; evil is the power that consumes. Love is like gentle waters, evil is like consuming fire. This is why fire frequently symbolizes evil. This is why fire is used to describe the eternal place of those that do not belong to God, that is, have not come to love Divine Love. Those that are not born-again of Divine Love are consumed by the fire of evil within them, which means that evil is like fire; a fire within that will consume you from within. Evil cannot be controlled. Eventually evil will consume its host. As a surgeon cuts out a tumor so evil must be eradicated from within you.

Matthew 5:29–30
If your right eye causes you to sin, gouge it out and throw it away. It is better for you to lose one part of your body than for your whole body to be thrown into hell. [30] And if your right hand causes you to sin, cut it off and throw it away. It is better for you to lose one part of your body than for your whole body to go into hell. (NIV84)

Jesus was speaking spiritual symbolic words here. He is talking about the importance of removing evil motives from yourself. He is not talking about actually gouging out an eye or cutting off a hand. Neither your eye nor your hand can do anything good or evil. It is you that animates both that must be controlled. If you are coveting things that you know that you should not covet or doing things that you know that you should not do, then take control and stop it now. That is what Jesus means here.

Please my friend, don't let evil deceive you into thinking that you can control it. Evil is seductive. Evil is like an addictive substance that someone is hooked on. The addicted person always hears the seductive call until they are completely done with it, now and forever, if that day ever comes. And also don't think that because you are not addicted to obvious addictive habits or substances that you have evil under control. Evil is also very subtle. Anything, and I mean anything, that draws you away from living a life of Divine Love is evil, and that evil thing is uncontrollable. It might not be obvious to you while you are living in the world, but when you depart the world and are completely away from

God's healing power, the evil within will quickly consume you.

We must not lose track of the fact that we are first and foremost, and essentially, only spirit beings, and that we only temporally live in selfish animal bodies. Our bodies will never lead us to God. Our bodies are selfish by design. They must be fed and they must be kept warm and they have a million other drives and desires, but we, who live within them, must keep our bodies in check. We must be masters of our bodies and take great care not to let our bodies dictate major things in our lives.

Romans 8:5–8
Those who live according to the sinful nature [human instincts] have their minds set on what that nature desires; but those who live in accordance with the Spirit have their minds set on what the Spirit [God] desires. [6] The mind of sinful man [human body focused] is death, but the mind controlled by the Spirit is life and peace; [7] the sinful mind [human body focused] is hostile to God. It does not submit to God's law, nor can it do so. [8] Those controlled by the sinful nature [human body] cannot please God. (NIV84)

Here is a relevant Scripture that I particularly like.

Matthew 11:12
From the days of John the Baptist until now, the kingdom of heaven has been forcefully advancing, and forceful men lay hold of it. (NIV84)

You must be in control of yourself. You must be a forceful person inside. You have to take charge of your body, and tell it what it can and cannot have. If you go with the flow, you will, in the end, be flushed. Evil flows down and the road to heaven is up. Do you understand the spiritual words I am using here? It is easier to flow down the river than to paddle up it. Only a determined person will keep paddling up the river to get to his destination. Only a forceful person will take hold of their life and make it do the right things.

I have an interesting thought on this topic of controlling the flesh. I don't know if it is true or not, but I think it is interesting. The controlling of our bodies is a difficult thing to do. When a person becomes possessed by an evil spirit, that spirit gains some form of control over your body. But, whatever is possessing said person doesn't seem to have the ability to control the body with any degree of subtly. What I mean, my observations on the matter indicate to me that a demon possessed person is never an athlete or even has basic control over the mind of its host. I think that

controlling a body is not the easiest thing to do and if you want to control yours you must work at it just like an athlete must thoroughly control his or hers if he or she wants to compete. Anyway, this is just a thought.

1 Corinthians 9:24–27
Do you not know that in a race all the runners run, but only one gets the prize? Run in such a way as to get the prize. [25] Everyone who competes in the games goes into strict training. They do it to get a crown that will not last; but we do it to get a crown that will last forever. [26] Therefore I do not run like a man running aimlessly; I do not fight like a man beating the air. [27] No, I beat my body and make it my slave so that after I have preached to others, I myself will not be disqualified for the prize. (NIV84)

Duty

F YOU ARE GOING TO play the game then I think that it is always best to know what the rules of the game are and what the true object of the game is. We are playing the Game of Life and most people are like chaff that the wind blows around. The Lord has allowed me to see and understand some of this and I will do my best to explain what I see in words.

If you and your spouse are obedient and god-fearing parents then you are going to want that your children grow up to be obedient and god-fearing people in their own right. No god-fearing parent will ever want their child to grow up as an evil person. The idea that all you want is for your children to be happy is totally bogus. What understanding parent could be happy with a happy child that is lost to evil and ends up in Hell? It just isn't possible. Any understanding parent wants what is best for their children.

Well, God wants the exact same thing for his children as the understanding parents wants for theirs.

So, this being true, what then is the duty of the understanding parents? Is it not to teach and train their children in the ways of right? Isn't that the moral obligation of any understanding parent? It is the moral obligation of the understanding parents to themselves be upright and obedient and moral. They must lead the way for their children. The proverb, Do as I say and not as I do, is a totally bogus proverb; is will never work. Your first obligation as a parent is for you yourself to be obedient to God, then you can expect your children to be first obedient to you and then to God.

When your children learn this obedience they will then grow up in to adults that are first obedient to God for the benefit of themselves and for the benefit of their own children. This is how things work.

Now, God is our parent, if we call him Father. And he is always holy and pure and obedient to Divine Love.

Philippians 2:5–11
Your attitude should be the same as that of Christ Jesus: [6] Who, being in very nature God, did not consider equality with God something to be grasped, [7] but made himself nothing, taking the very nature of a servant, being made in human likeness.
[8] And being found in appearance as a man, he humbled himself and became obedient to death— even death on a cross! [9] Therefore God exalted him to the highest place and gave him the name that is above every name, [10] that at the name of Jesus every knee should bow, in heaven and on earth and under the earth, [11] and every tongue confess that Jesus Christ is Lord, to the glory of God the Father.
(NIV84)

The duty of children, whether yourself to God, or your own children to you, is to obey and conform to the expectations of their parents regarding right conduct.

Someone once told me that children will rise to the level of expectation provided that the expectation is reasonable and the parents hold to the same level of behavior. I believe that this is true. A parent might want better for their child, but it is unrealistic to expect a higher moral level than you yourself are willing to conform too.

God showed us his level of obedience in Christ Jesus. God expects that we show the same level of obedience that he did. This is God's expectation with respect to you. This is a reasonable expectation, as he himself conformed to it. It is your duty to rise to the level of this expectation. God will never give up on you, so long as you never give up on meeting his expectations. I am not saying that you will rise to the perfect level of obedience that Jesus operated in, but you must try. That is how you grow. When you do reach the level of obedience that Jesus operated in, then you will be fully mature.

Ephesians 4:11–13
It was he who gave some to be apostles, some to be prophets, some to be evangelists, and some to be pastors and teachers, [12] to prepare God's people for works of service, so

that the body of Christ may be built up [13] **until we all reach unity in the faith and in the knowledge of the Son of God and become mature, attaining to the whole measure of the fullness of Christ.** (NIV84)

Now, God is Divine Love. God does not have a selfish bone in his body, so to say. God, himself, is the epitome of perfection, that is, he is Divine Love without limit and without deviation. He is in his completeness, all in all, Love. I am not saying this to win points with God. I am trying to establish the baseline of what God really and truly is. I am trying to show to you, my friend, what God actually is. I want you to see through the smoke that the world has obscured God with. If you were to meet God on the street you would have met a person of complete perfection in that he is completely love and has no selfishness in him. There is nothing that he wants anyone to do for him. There is nothing that anyone, or everyone, can do for God. Every thought and desire that God has for you is for your benefit. Even when the Bible tells you to worship God, it tells you this because for you to worship Divine Love is to value Divine Love above everything else. Do you understand what I am saying here? God doesn't need your worship to puff him up with? God can't be puffed up, he is Divine Love. Divine Love isn't about one's self. Not for God and not for you. If you love God then you love what is best, and what is eternal. If you do not love God then there is something wrong with you. If you don't love Divine Love then you probably love yourself. Who told you to do that? What makes you think that you are better than God? Or, do you hate God because you think that God will not have you? Do you shake your fist at God because you stand condemned? Foolish person, Divine Love always hopes for you. If you want proof that Divine Love desires you then look at Jesus. God sent his Son, a full expression of himself, and of the perfectly obedient man, to suffer death and deprivation and humiliation, all to provide a path by which you might be restored to him. Does someone devise a plan to save another, which requires their own death, unless love is behind it? Think about this; it is very important. God sent his Son Jesus Christ to be the Savior of the world. He did this so that every man, every woman, every child, might be born-again alive inside of God, so that the family of God might be filled with children of Divine Love. This is God's plan, and our duty as it were, is to take hold of God by way that he established.

Have you ever wondered why alcohol addicted people will drink themselves to death even when they know that it is killing them? Why

does anyone do a self-destructive act when they feel blue? It is because the enemy has convinced them that they are not worth God's affection, let alone love. They feel alone and abandoned. They just want a little comfort, so they do what they know is wrong because they get a little comfort out of it. A person that is caught in this self-destructive cycle doesn't know that God sent his only begotten Son to die on their behalf. They do not understand, or believe, that anyone could really and truly love them. But the Lord God Almighty can and will love anyone that comes and loves him. You see, my friend, it is impossible to truly love God and love sin at the same time. It is the person that does not love themselves that can love God. God desires that you love him; in fact he requires it, not because he needs your love and adoration, but rather because such love and adoration means that you have come to him to receive from him his love for you. God wants to love you and he wants you to love him. This is all so very difficult to explain. God does not desire your attention because he has a weakness within himself that needs bolstering by having followers. God is self-contained. He wants your love because he desires to have a love relationship with you. It is difficult for us to understand all of this, because we tend to think that others think the way that we do. If I want a beautiful woman to love me there is probably something down inside of me that wants it for me. I will get to caress her. I will get to look upon her and listen to the sound of her voice. Because I am evil I want things that I want for reasons that benefit me. But God does not think that way. There is nothing evil in him. If he wants you to love him, it is for your benefit and that is reason enough. God made man not because he needed company, but rather to share his love with. God made man so that man could partake in love.

When Jesus came to the earth he revealed many valuable and interesting things to us. Possibly the most important revelation that he brought to us was a new name for God for us. We saw this name before, as it relates to God, but Jesus really brought it home to us, as it were. God the Father; God who is the Father of his children and we the children of God; Jesus showed us that God the Creator of Heaven and Earth, desires to adopt us as his children, as it were. Wow.

Now, imagine that you are a pre-adolescent orphan child and you are destined for a life of suffering and death, but then some selfless person truly desires to have you come and be a part of his family. Imagine that you are now living in his loving home and are being cared for and loved without limit. Do you think that you have some duty or obligation to your

new family? Don't you see that you should let the family's love comfort and change you so that you can in turn express that love to others? God doesn't adopt people because they need it. God extends his love to you because he wants you to respond to that love and return it. He sees you in your abandoned orphan state and he says to you. **"Come to me, all you who are weary and burdened, and I will give you rest." Matthew 11:28 (NIV84).** He extends the invitation, but you must respond.

God wants children that are like him. Friends are fine, but God wants more. Symbolically God wants a wife like relationship with you; for you to be an intimate love companion. God is reaching down to pull you up, as it were. He sees you squirming around in the filth of sin and he wants you to grab hold of his extended arm and let him pull you out of the world's ways and into the way of Divine Love. Those that love the world aren't even looking for God; they do not see him; they do not hear him; they do not care about him. Those people that see the deficiency in themselves, and the beauty in God, eagerly grab hold of God's extended arm and rejoice in their salvation.

Once you see God, by faith, and respond to his call, then you have a duty to wash the filth from you and become a member of the family. You were pulled out of selfishness into a new being of Divine Love.

1 Corinthians 13:1–7
If I speak in the tongues of men and of angels, but have not love, I am only a resounding gong or a clanging cymbal. [2] If I have the gift of prophecy and can fathom all mysteries and all knowledge, and if I have a faith that can move mountains, but have not love, I am nothing. [3] If I give all I possess to the poor and surrender my body to the flames, but have not love, I gain nothing.
[4] Love is patient, love is kind. It does not envy, it does not boast, it is not proud. [5] It is not rude, it is not self-seeking, it is not easily angered, it keeps no record of wrongs. [6] Love does not delight in evil but rejoices with the truth. [7] It always protects, always trusts, always hopes, always perseveres. (NIV84)

This is God. God is not like this, but is this. The core of his being is love. Love looks outside the body and sustains. Love does not worry about itself; Love is a servant, love is incorruptible.

We saw before that when God created Satan he had created him perfect in beauty and full of wisdom but because of his beauty and wisdom he became proud and elevated his self-importance above his faith relation-

ship with God. This brought about unintended consequences for all those that followed in his footsteps. The force of the unintended consequences was evil. Evil is a cancer that consumes its host. Evil is what happens when you separate yourself from the Sustainer, that is, when you separate yourself from Divine Love. When self becomes your focus, as it were, self will want more and more until all that is left of you, is nothing. Self takes and takes from others until everyone is eating at each other and there is no peace. Self thinks in a vacuum but does not live in a vacuum. When you live in a community of self-centered beings, is it any surprise that it will consume itself? How could such beings exist forever, and ever, and ever and not corrupt everything around them?

Now, God created man in his own image and after his own likeness. Man ultimately is far more beautiful and potentially wise than Satan ever was. But God hid this beauty and wisdom from man so that man would not become prideful and think more of himself than he should. God wanted man to remain a love being. God wanted man to remain humble, and meek, and gentle, and kind, and patient and so forth, so God put his beloved children into humiliating animal bodies and prevented them from being able to see their own potential.

Now, my friend, once you understand this, then it all makes complete sense. Imagine that you, yourself had all of the qualities of the Spirit of God, and further imagine that you were the richest and most powerful person on earth, and imagine that you had children of your own; now wouldn't you teach your children to be loving, and kind, and gentle, and patient, and so on, so that they too would grow up to be like you, benefiting from love and not a victim of selfish evil? Given that God is the kind of person that he says that he is, is it any wonder that he desires that we should be like him? What I am trying to convey to you it that God is not trying to limit you, but rather he is trying to raise you up, to be a healthy and happy person. Man was created by God to be like God, in every way that is important. He created man to be his friend and fellowship partner.

I want you to imagine that you are the most powerful and richest man or woman on earth and that you are truly good inside and holy and pure. Imagine that you really and truly desire, and embrace those qualities, and that you are not secretly wicked inside. This is actually kind of hard to imagine, because most people try to look good on the outside but inside they want selfish things, things that excite them, things that make them hot. But please, for the sake of argument, imagine that you really are good,

through and through. Now, what kind of wife/husband would you want? Would you want someone that was like yourself, to help you raise your children, so that they too would grow up and embrace the qualities that you admire? Clearly you would. This is exactly what God wants too. It should be no surprise to you, if you have ever stopped and thought about it; it is just common sense.

Inside you there is a person that will never be at peace until it is in harmony with God. But, that person is hidden within a selfish body. That body wants all sorts of things. You, the person inside, must decide what you want ultimately. Do you want peace? Or do you want excitement? Have you ever gone out of your way to do something for someone else, a person that was a stranger and could never return the favor? If you have, do you remember what it felt like inside of you; a sort of quiet joy? That is what I am talking about here.

Through the Mirror Darkly

1 Corinthians 13:8–13
Love never fails. But where there are prophecies, they will cease; where there are tongues, they will be stilled; where there is knowledge, it will pass away. [9] For we know in part and we prophesy in part, [10] but when perfection comes, the imperfect disappears. [11] When I was a child, I talked like a child, I thought like a child, I reasoned like a child. When I became a man, I put childish ways behind me. [12] Now we see but a poor reflection as in a mirror; then we shall see face to face. Now I know in part; then I shall know fully, even as I am fully known. [13] And now these three remain: faith, hope and love. But the greatest of these is love. (NIV84)

HIS PASSAGE TELLS US THAT now we see spiritual things only dimly. When we see God in the Scriptures we only see a whisper, barely a glimmer, of his glory. We see his glory as in a shadow of his person and not face to face, so to say, truth is, in our present human bodies we couldn't handle God's glory full blast. Now we hear tell of his glory and magnificence, but we experience a tingling of a single hair. It is only by faith that we see and experience anything. But, this is a very important truth. It is important to our very lives. Satan and his angels could see God in all his glory and yet they still allowed pride to rise up within their selves and that pride poisoned them to death. Because they could actually see God's goodness, and still wanted separation from him, their sin was/is unforgiveable.

Again, imagine yourself married to a perfect husband/wife (a spouse that is nothing but good and true), and yet you go and cheat on him or her with a truly trashy person. How could your spouse have faith in you again once this betrayal was discovered? Imagine again, that you are truly an innocent and don't really understand goodness and evil, but in your innocence you abandoned your holy and pure spouse, and embraced the thrill of evil; do you think that your ignorance of the consequences would matter to your spouse? You, though you were innocent, looked at evil and desired it; desired it over holiness and purity. Adultery in this manner is unforgiveable, because you wanted that which was evil even though you had that which was good. A person must take control of oneself.

This is the state of things regarding the angels that sinned. Even though they did not understand the consequences of their action they nonetheless desired evil in the face of goodness. They were with goodness, and instead of loving it, they were bored and found goodness wanting. Please understand that my examples above are not about human husbands and wives. You, earthling, cannot see into the heart of your spouse. In our present spiritual state we can only see things vaguely.

Fortunately for us we cannot see the glory of God—yet. We live in such a place that we cannot really see good or evil clearly. We get hints of both but do not see either clearly for what they are. We can read in the Bible and see by faith a promised place of goodness and peace, but we can't actually touch it with our hands, so to say.

We can experience both good acts and evil acts here on earth. Here we can aspire to what our inner person truly wants. We can aspire to the place of goodness and peace or we can revel in self-indulgence. We can pick what we want. The world is easy to see and you can chase after the world if you want, or you can believe the promise of heaven and pursue it. Here we can see goodness and peace and gentleness and all of the qualities of God, by faith, in the Bible, and want that more than anything else that this world has to offer. Even if heaven weren't really truth, (I am not saying that it is not true) you can want its qualities so much, that you would rather die than live without them. You can do that. You can. You can by faith. It is the qualities themselves that you can have now, if you will take hold of yourself and keep yourself on the path.

I don't believe that you can really scare people into goodness with warnings of hell and damnation. I just don't think it works that way. Oh, you can frighten them a bit and that fear might keep them from running

rampant, but a person must have a sincere desire for peace for them to really shy away from the world and earnestly live for God. If a person that desires peace looks and sees the real world, they can believe the hope held out to them in the Gospel, and then in hope and with faith live for that which is coming.

In a world of Satans, a person of God would rather remain single than to marry one. A person of God would rather suffer hunger and cold and humiliation than to marry a world-centered person. What do you want, my friend, and how badly do you want it? The Bible is here to help you see what is really out there and what your options are. The Bible can give substance to your heart's desire and substance to put your faith in. That is what makes the Bible so very very important.

What I am trying to say, is that here, in the world, we can see what the world has to offer and through the Bible we can see what God has promised. We can see both, vaguely, and we can choose which destiny we want. But in both cases you must look past the obvious, you must look deep and hard at the realities that exist. Do you want the world and its temporary pleasures or do you believe the Bible and listen to it, and through it experience spiritual peace and joy?

The Cost

HAVE HEARD COUNTLESS TIMES THAT salvation is free. It has been described to me to be like a jewel that you find on the ground, and you just pick it up and put it in your pocket. This is just about the biggest lie that I have ever heard. If it were free then you could just pick it up—snap—like that. It is true that you can't purchase salvation, that is, you can't be good enough to make it into heaven. It is not obtainable by you. Not one of the angelic beings that turned from God can or will ever, be restored to heaven. But these things do not make it free. First off, God Almighty, in the person of Jesus Christ, suffered a painful and unjust death to provide it. The cost of reconciliation is incalculable. Let us look at what Jesus said concerning the cost.

Matthew 13:44–46
"The kingdom of heaven is like treasure hidden in a field. When a man found it, he hid it again, and then in his joy went and sold all he had and bought that field.
[45] "Again, the kingdom of heaven is like a merchant looking for fine pearls. [46] When he found one of great value, he went away and sold everything he had and bought it. (NIV84)

Two parables, right in a row, saying essentially the same thing, tell you

that this is important. Both parables tell you that the cost is everything that you own. That sounds pretty expensive to me. My friend, please do not treat what God is offering you lightly. The attitude of so-called Christians today makes me sick, and it makes the Lord sick too.

> **Revelation 3:14–16**
> **"To the angel of the church in Laodicea write: These are the words of the Amen, the faithful and true witness, the ruler of God's creation. ¹⁵ I know your deeds, that you are nei-ther cold nor hot. I wish you were either one or the other! ¹⁶ So, because you are lukewarm—neither hot nor cold—I am about to spit you out of my mouth.** (NIV84)

Does this sound wishy-washy to you? The Lord paid for your potential reconciliation with his blood and he expects some fire from you too.

If it is your desire to escape the world, and through this escape be acceptable to God, then your motivations for life must change. One moment you were living for your own pleasures, and in the next you changed direction and started living to please the Lord, or did you?

History tells us that in England, during the seventeenth and eighteenth centuries, the aristocracy had butlers, housekeepers, maids, cooks and other such staff, who devoted their lives to making their masters happy. I don't know how much truth there is in this "historical fact," but whether or not it is true, it still serves as an example of how we should relate to God. For us, the Lord is our master. For us, his word is law. For us, God is to be honored and served.

If you are the Lord's man/woman then be the best that you can be. You must forget your life and live for him. No one can tell you what this means, but you must nonetheless discover it and do it.

> **2 Timothy 2:4**
> **No one serving as a soldier gets involved in civilian af-fairs—he wants to please his commanding officer.** (NIV84)

What I mean is that every person is different, and God has given each of us different gifts and such, and we are to devote these gifts and abili-ties in our service to God.

> **1 Corinthians 12:4–11**
> **There are different kinds of gifts, but the same Spirit. ⁵ There are different kinds of service, but the same Lord. ⁶ There are different kinds of working, but the same God works all of them in all men.**
> **⁷ Now to each one the manifestation of the Spirit is given for**

the common good. **⁸ To one there is given through the Spirit the message of wisdom, to another the message of knowledge by means of the same Spirit, ⁹ to another faith by the same Spirit, to another gifts of healing by that one Spirit, ¹⁰ to another miraculous powers, to another prophecy, to another distinguishing between spirits, to another speaking in different kinds of tongues, and to still another the interpretation of tongues. ¹¹ All these are the work of one and the same Spirit, and he gives them to each one, just as he determines. (NIV84)**

I think the point of our service to God is one of worship. If we truly worship God then we will be glad to be of any service at all. Now, as I have said before, God doesn't need anything from you, or anybody else. God doesn't want you to be his servant because he wants servants. He wants you to want to be his servant, and he wants you to deny yourself worldly pleasures, in your effort to serve him. God wants you to want him. And, and this is a really big and, he wants you to do your service to him in secret, so that you get nothing from the world for having done it. This is really important because it is really easy to lie to yourself and convince yourself that what you are doing is for God, but in fact it is for yourself.

Matthew 6:1–6
"Be careful not to do your 'acts of righteousness' before men, to be seen by them. If you do, you will have no reward from your Father in heaven.
² "So when you give to the needy, do not announce it with trumpets, as the hypocrites do in the synagogues and on the streets, to be honored by men. I tell you the truth, they have received their reward in full. ³ But when you give to the needy, do not let your left hand know what your right hand is doing, ⁴ so that your giving may be in secret. Then your Father, who sees what is done in secret, will reward you.
⁵ "And when you pray, do not be like the hypocrites, for they love to pray standing in the synagogues and on the street corners to be seen by men. I tell you the truth, they have received their reward in full. ⁶ But when you pray, go into your room, close the door and pray to your Father, who is unseen. Then your Father, who sees what is done in secret, will reward you. (NIV84)

The point of what God wants you to do, is to test you, to determine what you really believe, not for God, but for you. God already knows everything about you, but you do not know even the first thing about yourself.

By faith you have seen heaven and hell and are frightened, good, but

what are you going to do about it? You claim to love the Lord, but do you? What is it about the Lord that you love?

I have seen many times, and I am sure you have too, people worshiping some rock star or other, and I see them imitating that performer. They show true worship in their actions; misdirected, but true. What is it about Jesus Christ that you desire to imitate in secret, so that nobody else knows? If you don't know the answer to this question then I suggest that you read the Bible more. Read it until you really and actually know him.

Two Families

THERE TWO FAMILIES OF MAN on the earth today. First are those that belong to God and also those that do not. Without any doubt the largest group is the group of world lovers.

It seems to me, from reading the Bible, and from looking around that the number of believers has always been pretty low (percentage wise). If I had to guess I would say, maybe, 100:1. That ratio might seem a bit low, but even if it is correct that would mean that there is more than five million believers in the world today. That is a lot of believers. There are probably more actual believers today than at any time before. Not because the world is a better place than in the past, but simply because the population of the earth is way more than it has ever been and the Bible has been distributed like never before.

This estimated ratio, if it is at all accurate, shows you why you should be very careful about listening to the opinions of others. If you polled a hundred people on the street chances are only one of them would actually and truly be a born-again believer. You would get, thereabouts, 99 worldly answers to just one spiritual answer, if that one believer that you chanced to meet happened to be one that was able to put into words the reasons for his or her faith. Please don't take these numbers and estimates as being at all reliable. There are so many factors that would have to be considered. Which country did you poll the people in? What was the age of the people? Are they city folk? Are the country folk? These questions go on and on and on. I am only trying to point out that there aren't very many believers in the world today and you must be careful about who you ask questions of. And you must be careful about listening to scientific studies that rely on population percentages.

One of the ways that the world works is that they like to make polls

and then they like to make statements about the meaning of the polls. One of my favorite poll results is the statistic that says that 98 percent of the world's population believes in God. Right. Oh, this next one is a funny one. Children are ninety percent more likely to be adopted by men rather than by women. That doesn't seem very likely does it? After listening to the reason however it becomes very likely indeed. The reason for this disparity is that most times women retain custody of their children in a divorce and their future husbands formally adopt their wife's children—simple.

My point is that you should be very careful about listening to statistics and the opinions of the general population. One might as well go down into Hell and ask the residents if God is fair.

The believers tend to be, more or less, invisible within the population. They are generally quiet and peaceful and don't put themselves forward. It is easy to discount them and to not notice them, but they are nonetheless there. I think, I don't know, but I think, that I am more noticeable than most of my true brothers and sisters. Those of us that have come to know the truth about the Bible and about God are obligated to share with others some of what we know. Is it possible for me to love my neighbor and not share something of what I know, given that I know how important it is to know?

Mark 4:21–25
He said to them, "Do you bring in a lamp to put it under a bowl or a bed? Instead, don't you put it on its stand? [22] For whatever is hidden is meant to be disclosed, and whatever is concealed is meant to be brought out into the open. [23] If anyone has ears to hear, let him hear."
[24] "Consider carefully what you hear," he continued. "With the measure you use, it will be measured to you—and even more. [25] Whoever has will be given more; whoever does not have, even what he has will be taken from him." (NIV84)

Jesus

ESUS IS BY FAR THE most important person ever to have lived on earth. Saying that statement is like saying that the sun is a bright light; it just doesn't say it. The more you know about the sun, the more amazing it becomes, and with Jesus Christ it is just like that. Compared to Jesus no one else, from the beginning to the end, is of any real importance whatsoever, historically speaking.

We have talked about how the sun represents God the Father, and how the moon symbolically represents Jesus, and how dark it is in the middle of the night, in the middle of a desert, on a moonless night. All of the stars, which represent all of the glory of each and every angel, are combined into pretty much nothing when compared to the light of the moon. And if the light of all of the angels is next to nothing then how much less is the illumination that man brings.

Jesus perfectly reflects the light from the Father into and on to this dark world. Jesus is like a reporter's video camera that has filmed a personal interview with the creator of the universe. Jesus is for man a window into God's soul. Can you now begin to see how important Jesus Christ is? No one else even remotely begins to shine such truth down on the earth. We have had philosophers, and wise men, and scientists, and teachers, and scholars, and what have you, but Jesus' vision is unique and totally accurate. Everyone else is guessing, but Jesus has been there and back and there again. Everyone else sees through the mirror darkly, but Jesus has been there face to face.

Mankind is sometimes compared to all of the sand on the shores of the earth; so how much light do they emit compared to the moon? A grain of sand emits no light so when compared to Jesus, a man, any man, is as the Bible says, dust on the scales. It just doesn't matter what any man thinks, not one little bit. Every man is in total darkness unless he has been taught some truth from the Lord God Almighty, and Jesus is truth personified, or as the Bible says, is Christ.

Without the revelation of God found in the person of Jesus Christ and in the Bible we would know nothing about God. We are just that cut off from spiritual knowledge. Without Jesus and the Bible we would have nothing but speculations and imaginations. Jesus Christ is our window into the person of God and that makes him so very important.

Who Is He?

Isaiah 9:1-2
Nevertheless, there will be no more gloom for those who were in distress. In the past he humbled the land of Zebulun and the land of Naphtali, but in the future he will honor Galilee of the Gentiles, by the way of the sea, along the Jordan—The people walking in darkness have seen a great

light; on those living in the land of the shadow of death a light has dawned. (NIV84)

s Jesus went about his ministry, speaking to the people of Galilee, he fulfilled this prophecy of Isaiah. This same truth applies to everyone on the earth, then as it is today, that as they are living their lives ignorant of God and of spiritual truth, that when they see and hear Jesus, in the Scriptures, they are seeing a Great Light, or they are seeing Spiritual Truth. Jesus is a walking and talking manifestation of the Truth. This cannot be said of any other person. Every single recorded word of Jesus, and every single action he did, is as though you were hearing and watching God Almighty himself in the body of a man.

Isaiah 9:6–7
For to us a child is born, to us a son is given, and the government will be on his shoulders. And he will be called Wonderful Counselor, Mighty God, Everlasting Father, Prince of Peace.
⁷ Of the increase of his government and peace there will be no end. He will reign on David's throne and over his kingdom, establishing and upholding it with justice and righteousness from that time on and forever. The zeal of the Lord Almighty will accomplish this. (NIV84)

This prophecy is about Jesus Christ. Look at Jesus' names. Jesus is the Wonderful Counselor; Jesus is the Mighty God; Jesus is the Everlasting Father; Jesus is the Prince of Peace. Jesus is important. To say that Jesus is important is like saying that the universe is big. Yes, the universe is big and yes Jesus is important.

Son of God

Mark 1:1
The beginning of the gospel about Jesus Christ, the Son of God. (NIV84)

esus is frequently called the Son of God in the Scriptures. If God the Father had a Son that was a chip off the old block that son would be Jesus. Jesus, in his earthly incarnation, is not greater than the Father, but is the perfect, and the obedient, son of God.

Jesus is not an actual son of God in the human sense. Using modern terminology we might say that Jesus was the perfect clone of God. It is like God cloned his spirit being, that is, his soul, and then he put that cloned self into the body of unborn baby, and then that baby grew up into

the man Jesus Christ. As I have talked about before, every man is really a spirit being that is temporally inside of a human body. Jesus is just like that too. Jesus is just like any other man in that he is a spirit person that is inside of a human body, however, the spirit person that Jesus is, is God. How did God do this? I haven't a clue. I don't know how God puts any of us within the bodies that we find ourselves within. This is an unrevealed mystery. The how is unrevealed, but the fact is not unrevealed.

The fact of the person of Jesus Christ is very important to us—obviously. What it means to us is that we can look at Jesus and listen to him, knowing that what he is saying and doing is the perfect will of God. If you look at any other person, who knows what you might be seeing, but when you look at Jesus you can know what you are seeing. If you look at any other historical figure you are not looking at God. In fact, there is no other historical figure that you can reliably look at, at all. The Bible is unparalleled in its preservation. We owe our very lives to the Israelite people for preserving the Old Testament Scriptures for us, and to the church fathers for preserving the New Testament. Through these writings we can see Jesus the Son of God.

Son of Man

NOTHER COMMON NAME FOR JESUS is Son of Man. This name is a reference to the fact that although he is God inside in his spirit person, he is also a man, through and through. This name also means that Jesus was born as a baby and raised on earth to grow into a man. An important thing to understand is that Jesus did not attain the status of a Son of God, and a Son of Man, he was born with this status. This is significant and important. Jesus is from God and as such this is God's plan. He was not some man that somehow made himself worthy of the titles. Jesus is not an example of what we can attain by effort, no; he is what he is, because God sent him to do what he did.

> **Isaiah 7:14**
> **Therefore the Lord himself will give you a sign: The virgin will be with child and will give birth to a son, and will call him Immanuel. (NIV84)**

This prophecy is not about the mother, but rather about the Son. Jesus was the Son of Man, yes, but he was not a descendent of man, but rather a 'descendent' of God directly. This is important because that which is evil cannot bring forth that which is holy. The distinction here is very important and concerns the legal status of Jesus in the spiritual world.

Satan has authority over everyone that is a son of sin, which until Jesus, was everyone born of a woman on earth. But, because Jesus was not a descendent of fallen man he was not in any way subject to Satan. Satan could do absolutely nothing to Jesus unless God allowed it. Nothing. Satan tried to kill Jesus soon after his birth, but God hid him away. And right after announcing his mission Satan tried again.

> **Luke 4:28–30**
> **All the people in the synagogue were furious when they heard this. [29] They got up, drove him out of the town, and took him to the brow of the hill on which the town was built, in order to throw him down the cliff. [30] But he walked right through the crowd and went on his way. (NIV84)**

Also see John 7:30 and 8:20.

Word of God

I HAVE MENTIONED THIS BEFORE BUT it is so important that I will say it again. Jesus Christ the Son of God was/is the Bible in human form. Both the Bible and Jesus are physical manifestations of God the Father in the world, so that we can see God and know his will. Without the Bible, we would not be able to see Jesus, and without Jesus we would not be able to see God. The whole Bible, not just the Gospels, is God made visible. There is much of God that was made visible to us that was made visible apart from the person of Jesus Christ the human man. I think that red letter editions of the Bible are wrong. They suggest that Jesus' words recorded in the Gospels carry more authority than the rest of the Bible and that is just not true. You do treat his words differently because they are spoken from God directly to us and as such we interpret them differently, but the whole Bible is given to us by revelation from the Spirit of God including the words of Jesus Christ. You must use wisdom in interpreting what I am writing to you here.

The Reason He Came

BEFORE THE COMING OF THE Son of God, God had been revealing himself and his will, formally, through various persons for about 1,500 years. Moses was the first of a long line of men that received revelation directly from God, and then put that revelation down on paper so that we might have an accurate record of supremely important information. Can there be anything more important to us than to have God's very own revelations recorded for us?

Deuteronomy 8:3
He humbled you, causing you to hunger and then feeding
you with manna, which neither you nor your fathers had
known, to teach you that man does not live on bread alone
but on every word that comes from the mouth of the LORD.
(NIV84)

Spiritual food is every bit as important as earthly food, more important actually.

Jesus came to us and told us many things, but any other prophet could have told us the same things, so why did Jesus come to us in the flesh? Clearly he had to come in the flesh for a reason other than to bring us revelation knowledge.

After Adam every single man, woman and child, was born under the curse that came upon Adam and his descendants because of his rebellious act. Adam broke faith with God and each and every one of his descendants suffered from the same separation. To be connected to God is life; to be separated from God is death. That which is dead cannot spontaneously come to life again. That which is alive is alive and that which is dead is dead. Even in our world dead things cannot give birth to living things. A seed comes from a living plant and is alive when it grows into another living plant. If you were to kill that seed with radiation it could never thereafter sprout into a new living plant. The life in a living seed is dormant, but it is there. It is alive. That is why it can later sprout and grow.

Scientists love to play at making things grow, but never, and I totally mean never, will any man ever be able to create life. Scientist can only manipulate living things into life.

God is the source of life and no living thing can ever come into existence apart from its connection to God.

When the man, in the Garden, broke the faith-bond with God he became spiritually dead, that is, separated from God. There is nothing that man can ever do to fix this situation. Dead things cannot become alive things, apart from the direct will of God.

Matthew 19:23–26
Then Jesus said to his disciples, "I tell you the truth, it is
hard for a rich man to enter the kingdom of heaven. ²⁴ Again

> **I tell you, it is easier for a camel to go through the eye of a needle than for a rich man to enter the kingdom of God."**
> **²⁵ When the disciples heard this, they were greatly astonished and asked, "Who then can be saved?"**
> **²⁶ Jesus looked at them and said, "With man this is impossible, but with God all things are possible." (NIV84)**

"Who then can be saved?" "With man this is impossible, ..." With man restoration from death to life is impossible. There is no possible way for you to be reconnected to God by anything that you can ever do. It is impossible. For man it is impossible, but not for God, for anything is possible for God. God can choose to reconnect you to himself, but what about the fact that God is also just? Can God be just and still forgive and forget?

> **Revelation 12:10**
> **Then I heard a loud voice in heaven say:**
> **"Now have come the salvation and the power and the kingdom of our God, and the authority of his Christ. For the accuser of our brothers, who accuses them before our God day and night, has been hurled down. (NIV84)**

Here we see that Satan is called "**the accuser of our brother**". Satan is the finger-pointer. "Look at what he just did!" says, the Devil. Satan stands before God and basically says to God that "You can't judge me for what I did unless you judge them for what they are doing."

The Judge of heaven and earth must be just.

> **2 Samuel 14:14**
> **Like water spilled on the ground, which cannot be recovered, so we must die. But God does not take away life; instead, he devises ways so that a banished person may not remain estranged from him. (NIV84)**

I totally love this verse. Man is cut off from God and must surely die, but God devises ways so that man might not remain estranged from him.

For the heavenly beings that broke faith with God there is no salvation possible. What that means is that there is no way to bring them back into a faith relationship with the All Mighty. They broke faith with God with their eyes opened, so to say.

> **Hebrews 6:4–6**
> **It is impossible for those who have once been enlightened, who have tasted the heavenly gift, who have shared in the Holy Spirit, ⁵ who have tasted the goodness of the word of God and the powers of the coming age, ⁶ if they fall away,**

to be brought back to repentance, because to their loss they are crucifying the Son of God all over again and subjecting him to public disgrace. (NIV84)

This verse is talking about born-again people that fall away from God, but it has application to the heavenly beings too. This is talking about seeing God for what he is and then thinking that you can do better. Can you do better? Are you better than God? Forget about the whole power aspect of God; are you morally superior to God?

Mark 3:28–29
I tell you the truth, all the sins and blasphemies of men will be forgiven them. ²⁹ But whoever blasphemes against the Holy Spirit will never be forgiven; he is guilty of an eternal sin." (NIV84)

If a man, with his eyes open, sins against God then there is no hope for that man. This was the situation for Judas after he betrayed the Lord Jesus Christ to the rulers in Jerusalem. This is the situation for each and every heavenly being that broke away from God. But, this is not the case for man in general. God hid man in bodies of clay; bodies that were almost incapable of seeing the spiritual world. It turns out that the very liability of our very poor spiritual vision is really an asset, at least for now it is an asset. We cannot see the glory of God, so it is very difficult for us to blaspheme against God. This is no accident. This is also something that Satan didn't really understand. Satan could see God in all of his glory, but man could not.

Satan could and would point out to God man's sin, but man's accountability was something that Satan couldn't really grasp. Satan's understanding of our situation wasn't much better than our own understanding of his situation.

As the wise woman said in Samuel above, God devises ways in which an estranged person might be restored to him. God is totally and completely intelligent. No plan of God's can fail. God devised a plan that Satan couldn't understand, but that man could understand. You must understand that the whole physical universe is a mystery to Satan, and to all of the heavenly host for that matter.

1 Peter 1:10–12
Concerning this salvation, the prophets, who spoke of the grace that was to come to you, searched intently and with the greatest care, ¹¹ trying to find out the time and circumstances to which the Spirit of Christ in them was pointing when he predicted the sufferings of Christ and the glo-

ries that would follow. ¹²It was revealed to them that they were not serving themselves but you, when they spoke of the things that have now been told you by those who have preached the gospel to you by the Holy Spirit sent from heaven. Even angels long to look into these things. (NIV84)

Did you notice that last sentence? We are dealing with a mystery here. The meaning of it is hidden. Is it any wonder that it is not obvious to you either? If Satan can't figure it out do you think that it would be as clear as day for us?

It was necessary for this plan to be hidden from Satan but understandable to us. Look at this…

1 Corinthians 2:8
None of the rulers of this age understood it, for if they had, they would not have crucified the Lord of glory. (NIV84)

The rulers in this passage are spiritual rulers, Satan and his cohorts. Let's look at this whole passage.

1 Corinthians 2:6–16
We do, however, speak a message of wisdom among the mature, but not the wisdom of this age or of the rulers of this age, who are coming to nothing. ⁷No, we speak of God's secret wisdom, a wisdom that has been hidden and that God destined for our glory before time began. ⁸None of the rulers of this age understood it, for if they had, they would not have crucified the Lord of glory. ⁹However, as it is written: "No eye has seen, no ear has heard, no mind has conceived what God has prepared for those who love him"— ¹⁰but God has revealed it to us by his Spirit.
The Spirit searches all things, even the deep things of God. ¹¹For who among men knows the thoughts of a man except the man's spirit within him? In the same way no one knows the thoughts of God except the Spirit of God. ¹²We have not received the spirit of the world but the Spirit who is from God, that we may understand what God has freely given us. ¹³This is what we speak, not in words taught us by human wisdom but in words taught by the Spirit, expressing spiritual truths in spiritual words. ¹⁴The man without the Spirit does not accept the things that come from the Spirit of God, for they are foolishness to him, and he cannot understand them, because they are spiritually discerned. ¹⁵

The spiritual man makes judgments about all things, but he himself is not subject to any man's judgment:
[16] "For who has known the mind of the Lord that he may instruct him?"
But we have the mind of Christ. (NIV84)

This plan of God, this salvation for man, is a hidden mystery that was accomplished by Jesus Christ. Jesus did what had to be done and made salvation possible. Jesus did this in a way that Satan didn't understand. Had Satan understood, he never would have crucified Jesus.

So, let us move along and look at Jesus and what he did.

Matthew 1:18–21
This is how the birth of Jesus Christ came about: His mother Mary was pledged to be married to Joseph, but before they came together, she was found to be with child through the Holy Spirit. [19] Because Joseph her husband was a righteous man and did not want to expose her to public disgrace, he had in mind to divorce her quietly.
[20] But after he had considered this, an angel of the Lord appeared to him in a dream and said, "Joseph son of David, do not be afraid to take Mary home as your wife, because what is conceived in her is from the Holy Spirit. [21] She will give birth to a son, and you are to give him the name Jesus, because he will save his people from their sins." (NIV84)

We see here information about the conception of Jesus. We see that no man had any part in it. This is very important, and I imagine that Satan didn't appreciate the significance of this either. I am sure that he understood some of it, but not the whole of it. That is how things are hidden in the Bible. The obvious truth, the virgin conception and birth, are understandable by anyone, but the reason for it that is not so easily understood. The person that should not understand understands some and thinks that is all, but there is more.

So, what we have in Jesus was a sinless man; a man this is not descended from a man of sin, but descended from the Sinless God. This is the significant thing. The virgin birth was only a means of bringing the sinless man into being. Everyone looks at the obvious miracle and misses the important significance of it all. Jesus being born completely sinless meant that Satan had no hold over him whatsoever. Satan knew that he was a sinless man, and that he had no hold over Jesus, so the obvious solution for Satan was either to kill Jesus or corrupt Jesus, as he had corrupted the previous sinless man (Adam).

Satan then made several attempts to kill Jesus, and failed, because, again, he had no hold over him. And so we come to the temptation of Christ. Here we see Satan's attempt to corrupt Jesus as he had corrupted man before.

Now, remember, sin is all about self. There is Divine Love and there is self. There is God and there is you. That's pretty simple. Get Jesus to do something for himself and you have him.

Matthew 4:3
The tempter came to him and said, "If you are the Son of God, tell these stones to become bread." (NIV84)

Jesus knew who he was, but this is more subtle than that. Jesus is in the desert, and has been fasting for 40 days and nights, and is hungry (understatement I am sure) and the tempter tells him to command the stones to become bread. This is something that I am sure Jesus could have done (thus the temptation) and Jesus says no. He says…

Matthew 4:4
Jesus answered, "It is written: 'Man does not live on bread alone, but on every word that comes from the mouth of God.'" (NIV84)

Jesus quotes a Scripture from Deuteronomy to Satan, saying that he is totally God's servant and that God will provide for him. This is how we battle with Satan my friend. We don't fight him in our own power because he is more powerful than us, but we instead fight him with God's word and in that way God is fighting him and not us at all. When Satan brings a temptation to you, fight him with God's word.

Matthew 4:5–7
Then the devil took him to the holy city and had him stand on the highest point of the temple. ⁶ "If you are the Son of God," he said, "throw yourself down. For it is written:
" 'He will command his angels concerning you, and they will lift you up in their hands, so that you will not strike your foot against a stone.'"
⁷ Jesus answered him, "It is also written: 'Do not put the Lord your God to the test.'" (NIV84)

Jesus fought him with Scripture the first time and so Satan tries to trick Jesus with Scripture himself, but to no avail because Jesus doesn't just know the Scriptures, but the Scriptures are alive within his heart (as they should be in you too).

Luke 4:5–8
The devil led him up to a high place and showed him in an instant all the kingdoms of the world. ⁶ And he said to him, "I will give you all their authority and splendor, for it has been given to me, and I can give it to anyone I want to. ⁷ So if you worship me, it will all be yours."
⁸ Jesus answered, "It is written: 'Worship the Lord your God and serve him only.'" (NIV84)

I find this to be the most interesting of the three temptations. What I find so interesting is the fact that Satan tells us that all of the earth's kingdoms belong to him. So, when we see the statue that represents all of the relevant kingdoms in Daniel chapter two, that statue is also a representation of the person of Satan. Interesting. As the kingdoms progress through time from Babylon to the Roman, we see a progression of less and less nobility and more and more cruelty. Interesting. This is a picture of sin's effect on Satan over time. Also interesting. Satan offers the world to Jesus, but Jesus says to Satan that God will give to him what God wills and that will always be good enough. Are you, my friend, one hundred percent content with what God will give to you?

Recapping a bit, we see Jesus Christ, the sinless man, being brought forth into the world. Satan recognizes the danger and tries to kill Jesus and then to corrupt him, but fails on both accounts. Let's move on.

Luke 4:17–21
The scroll of the prophet Isaiah was handed to him. Unrolling it, he found the place where it is written: ¹⁸
"The Spirit of the Lord is on me, because he has anointed me to preach good news to the poor. He has sent me to proclaim freedom for the prisoners and recovery of sight for the blind, to release the oppressed, ¹⁹ to proclaim the year of the Lord's favor."
²⁰ Then he rolled up the scroll, gave it back to the attendant and sat down. The eyes of everyone in the synagogue were fastened on him, ²¹ and he began by saying to them, "Today this scripture is fulfilled in your hearing." (NIV84)

This Scripture that Jesus quoted says so much. It tells us what Jesus' mission was. He was to proclaim to the people Satan's defeat and God's victory. He then told them that that very day this Scripture was fulfilled in their hearing. He did not tell them that the Devil had been defeated, but rather that he would be defeated. That was what he was proclaiming. But, what was Satan to think after hearing this? Remember, that Satan doesn't really understand what is going on here. He sees Jesus, whom

he has no control over, making this proclamation and then also sees him going around healing people and setting them free from Satan's power by the power of faith, which is something that Satan also doesn't really understand. The puzzle here for Satan is how these defeated people, these obvious "sinners" could have faith to be set free from anything. Satan is pointing out the people's sins, but God isn't paying attention. What's up with that, Satan wonders? These people are guilty of far worse sins than Satan, and yet God is being friendly with them. How is that possible? Satan doesn't know.

When Satan and his angels elevated themselves above the God of Love, they by their own design, were no longer subject to Divine Love and so they were excluded from the sphere of Love's dominion. Satan and his angels thought that they could make for themselves a better place to live, a place more designed for self, a place that would be more of a place of pleasure. What Satan didn't understand was that for eternity to work it must be ruled by Divine Love. Self is a cancer that consumes its hosts. When Satan and his angels broke away from God, that is, broke the faith-bond with God, they were then unable to mend the broken faith-bond and were therefore left to their own resources with which to build their existence. To live with God is to be faith-bonded to the God of Peace, Harmony and Continuity. This is very hard to describe. To live with God means that you are with him in his Love, that is, you must have faith in God, that is, faith in Love, Peace, Faithfulness, Kindness, Patience, Gentleness, Joy and Self-Control. When you have faith in these fruits then you don't look for a more Self-gratifying way of life. If you believe in God then you believe in God. It is not possible to believe in something that you do not believe in. It is God that holds us in our unbelief and draws us to him and changes us so that we can believe. It is God that shows us the fallacy of our beliefs so that we can see and understand the way of God.

The spirit beings that broke faith with God were unable to mend their broken faith, because they were unfaithful in full view of God. Such an act of unfaithfulness causes a condition called spiritual death. Once you are dead, you are dead, and can do nothing to reconnect yourself to God. If you were to cheat on your spouse how could you be made clean again? Once soiled you cannot make yourself clean again. It is impossible. When those angels put their faith in Satan they were soiled and impure, they had no way to become holy and pure again. This resulted in their eternal separation from God. They were then free to exist apart from God, and in fact, they must thereafter exist apart from God.

All of this happened before God created the heavens and the earth.

Genesis 1:1
In the beginning God created the heavens and the earth.
(NIV84)

In the beginning of time, God created the earth with its atmosphere and this within the universe. Before the universe was built there was no beginning. A beginning requires time; something that doesn't exist in Heaven. Did you notice that this passage says 'heavens' and not heaven. This is important. The heavens that it is referring to are first the sky and then outer space.

After the angels rebelled God created the heavens and the earth, a place where fallen beings could live. But, at that time the rule of the world was turned over to man, holy and righteous man, spiritually alive man, un-fallen man. Man had divinely ordained authority to rule. Satan did not have any authority and at that time the world did not belong to him.

Genesis 3:1
Now the serpent was more crafty than any of the wild animals the LORD God had made. (NIV84)

We see more spiritual language here. The serpent is symbolic for Satan and the words, wild animals, as opposed to cultivated or domesticated animals, that is, animals that cannot live in harmony with God, are symbolic for the fallen angels and any beings that are not in harmony with God. What we are seeing here is that this crafty being, Satan, set about to con the woman into breaking faith with God. The woman listened to Satan and did break faith with God and then the man sided with her over God. The woman was deceived and the man was not.

After man broke the faith-bond with God he found that his connection to God was broken. The whole of creation became subject to Satan, the head of all of the fallen. This was a victory for Satan, but actually a hollow victory. It was a hollow victory because it was only a temporary victory. As I said before, Satan didn't fully understand this creation and how it works. Satan didn't really understand the dual nature of man and how the inner man can have a different destiny than the outer man. This was all new to him and he just didn't get it. Even after six thousand years very few understand much of this.

I am sure that Satan thought that when he brought about the fall of man in the Garden that man would be eternally separated from God as he was, but that was not what happened. I am sure that Satan was dumbfounded

with this when he saw God walking in the Garden right after the fall, and then God was reestablishing a bond with fallen man. Remember my friend there were at that time no Scriptures written at all. All Satan knew was that he was separated from God because of his rebellion and so he must have figured that if he could induce an act of rebellion from man, that man too would be in a like state. And then Satan, by virtue of his superior knowledge and understanding would be able to rule. This was Satan's plan, but it was a plan built on sand.

This brings us to something that is very important to understand and that is that the fall of man was never, not even for the briefest moments, an unexpected event for God. Nothing, and I mean nothing, is unexpected by God. God does not ever operate in Damage Control Mode. Everything was anticipated and so God built into his creation a way to fix the fall of man. God knew that the angels would fall and that man would also fall, long before (if before has meaning in eternity) either was created.

God built a loophole into the physical universe. He built it in such a way that man could not effectively see the Glory of God and so could not be held fully accountable for blaspheming it. Satan and his angels could clearly see God and so what they did was with open eyes, so to say, but man lived in a closed off place, so to say, and hadn't really a clue about glory.

Hebrews 6:4–6
It is impossible for those who have once been enlightened, who have tasted the heavenly gift, who have shared in the Holy Spirit, ⁵ who have tasted the goodness of the word of God and the powers of the coming age, ⁶ if they fall away, to be brought back to repentance, because to their loss they are crucifying the Son of God all over again and subjecting him to public disgrace. (NIV84)

When you think about this you can see that this is the exact situation that we see with our own children. When they are born they know almost nothing. We forgive them their folly because we know that they do not know. But, when they become adults and if then they reject sound morals then that is a different matter. We are God's children and we know next to nothing too, at least until God makes things truly known to us, then we are accountable to the things that we know.

James 3:1
Not many of you should presume to be teachers, my broth-

ers, because you know that we who teach will be judged more strictly. (NIV84)

So, we see that our world, the whole universe, was created by God to be a place to raise his children that would fall, so that he could teach them right from wrong, so that they would reject self-centeredness and choose God-centeredness, that is, love. They would willingly make this choice because they saw the effect of sin and the goodness of God. They could see sin directly and see by faith, heaven, and after having seen both they could, and some would, choose life over death.

So, looking back at Jesus we see on the one hand he was preaching the good news to the poor and was proclaiming freedom for the prisoners and recovery of sight for the blind and was showing the way for the oppressed to be released, and on the other hand he was preparing to defeat the Devil.

Matthew 16:21–23
From that time on Jesus began to explain to his disciples that he must go to Jerusalem and suffer many things at the hands of the elders, chief priests and teachers of the law, and that he must be killed and on the third day be raised to life.
²² Peter took him aside and began to rebuke him. "Never, Lord!" he said. "This shall never happen to you!"
²³ Jesus turned and said to Peter, "Get behind me, Satan! You are a stumbling block to me; you do not have in mind the things of God, but the things of men." (NIV84)

This is a pretty interesting Scripture. Jesus had been explaining that he was going to be killed in Jerusalem and Peter basically said no way Jose, this will never happen to YOU. What Peter did was a very natural thing for a human to say and do, but Jesus blew him away by calling him Satan. Jesus then explained his remark. He explained that Peter was thinking selfishly and should have been thinking of what God wanted. This was a lapse on Peter's part. He believed in Jesus and yet for a moment he was thinking like a man. He went from believing every word that Jesus spoke, to what he personally wanted, that is, he wanted Jesus to remain on earth and to establish his kingdom on earth; something that I want too. It is okay to want something, but quite another to go around God to get it. The Lord God always knows best.

To believe in Jesus does not mean to believe that he existed, and the same applies to God. Satan and the fallen angels all believe in God's existence, but none of them believe in God. To believe in Jesus (God)

is to believe that every single word will be fulfilled and that he is doing the exact right thing—always.

John 7:3–5
Jesus' brothers said to him, "You ought to leave here and go to Judea, so that your disciples may see the miracles you do. ⁴ No one who wants to become a public figure acts in secret. Since you are doing these things, show yourself to the world." ⁵ For even his own brothers did not believe in him. (NIV84)

In this passage Jesus' brothers were telling Jesus what he should do. My friend, you do not tell Jesus what to do, because whatever he is doing is the will of God, and to tell him what to do is to tell the Father what to do. Yikes.

Matthew 14:25–29
During the fourth watch of the night Jesus went out to them, walking on the lake. ²⁶ When the disciples saw him walking on the lake, they were terrified. "It's a ghost," they said, and cried out in fear. ²⁷ But Jesus immediately said to them: "Take courage! It is I. Don't be afraid."
²⁸ "Lord, if it's you," Peter replied, "tell me to come to you on the water."
²⁹ "Come," he said. Then Peter got down out of the boat, walked on the water and came toward Jesus. (NIV84)

The interesting part of this Scripture is not that Jesus walked on water. I figure that Jesus can do anything. No, the interesting part to me is what Peter said and did. He sees what he thinks is a ghost out on the water and is terrified, but then the Lord tells them in the boat not to be afraid, that it is only him, and then Peter says, Lord, it if it is you tell me to come to you on the water. Wow! Peter knew that if it were Jesus, and if Jesus said it, then it would happen. That is believing in Jesus.

On several occasions we see that Jesus told his disciples that he would be killed in Jerusalem and buried and on the third day rise, he was showing us that he was not a martyr, for a martyr is killed against his will for his beliefs, but Jesus was offering himself as a sacrifice. Jesus was the major participator in a plan by God to defeat the power of death, that is, separation from God. As long as people kept on sinning, Satan (the "accuser of the brothers") would point out each person's sin to God and make his claim, that is, Satan would say to God, "If I and my angels were excluded from heaven because of sin then you must exclude your precious man too."

Revelation 12:10
For the accuser of our brothers, who accuses them before our God day and night, has been hurled down. (NIV84)

So we see that, Jesus, the sinless man, went to Jerusalem to be offered as a sin offering to God, but Satan didn't know or understand this. What Satan thought was that Jesus was going to continue to grow in popularity until he united all of the people and established his kingdom on earth where Satan would have no power.

John 11:48
If we let him go on like this, everyone will believe in him, and then the Romans will come and take away both our place and our nation." (NIV84)

In this passage we see the leaders of the people voice their concerns. These people were Satan's people and the concern was Satan's. Satan was not worried about the Romans because he had the Romans in his pocket, so to say, but rather the world order which the Romans represented. In the prophecies it is the Roman Empire that is destroyed in the book of Revelation and after its destruction the Lord's kingdom on earth is establish during which Satan has been dethroned and is held in Hell. Satan is concerned about that. He sees Jesus as a real threat, the only real threat, to his earthly kingdom and power. Satan sees this and he wants desperately to get Jesus out of the way, and so he falls into God's trap.

John 13:21–28
After he had said this, Jesus was troubled in spirit and testified, "I tell you the truth, one of you is going to betray me." ²² His disciples stared at one another, at a loss to know which of them he meant. ²³ One of them, the disciple whom Jesus loved, was reclining next to him. ²⁴ Simon Peter motioned to this disciple and said, "Ask him which one he means."
²⁵ Leaning back against Jesus, he asked him, "Lord, who is it?"
²⁶ Jesus answered, "It is the one to whom I will give this piece of bread when I have dipped it in the dish." Then, dipping the piece of bread, he gave it to Judas Iscariot, son of Simon. ²⁷ As soon as Judas took the bread, Satan entered into him.
"What you are about to do, do quickly," Jesus told him, ²⁸ but no one at the meal understood why Jesus said this to him. (NIV84)

Notice, carefully, that it was Satan that entered into Judas to have Jesus

arrested and condemned. Judas did not want Jesus to be condemned. In fact, when he saw that Jesus had been condemned he was filled with such remorse that he killed himself. This was Satan's doing. Satan, who is called the god of this world, had Jesus arrested, condemned and killed.

> **Deuteronomy 21:22–23**
> **If a man guilty of a capital offense is put to death and his body is hung on a tree, [23] you must not leave his body on the tree overnight. Be sure to bury him that same day, because anyone who is hung on a tree is under God's curse. You must not desecrate the land the LORD your God is giving you as an inheritance.** (NIV84)

> **Galatians 3:13**
> **Christ redeemed us from the curse of the law by becoming a curse for us, for it is written: "Cursed is everyone who is hung on a tree."** (NIV84)

These scriptures tell us that if anyone is killed and hung up on a tree, as Jesus was (the cross was wood), that they have a curse from God on them. But, there is something hidden going on here that Satan did not understand, and that was that Jesus willingly accepted God's curse, even though he was not actually cursed himself, because he never ever sinned. Jesus willingly offered himself, and that was something that selfish Satan could not see coming. Satan thought that Jesus had, at some point, committed some sin or other. Satan had the power of death, but only over those that had sinned, because sin causes death. Satan did not have power over God, and he did not have power over Jesus, even though he thought he did.

While Jesus was on the cross, before he died, God put our sins on him. God draped sins on Jesus like one might drape dirty rags on a perfectly clean person's body. This is why Jesus quoted the first line of Psalm 22 while in the cross.

> **Matthew 27:46**
> **About the ninth hour Jesus cried out in a loud voice, *"Eloi, Eloi, lama sabachthani?"*—which means, "My God, my God, why have you forsaken me?"** (NIV84)

While Jesus was on the cross, God hid his face from him, just as he hides his face from any who willingly sin. God was treating Jesus like Jesus had forsaken him, but you and I know that Jesus never forsook God. This was all an elaborate ruse. God had a plan and Jesus in his perfect obedience was willing to participate in the plan, even though it called for an agonizing and humiliating death on a cross, one of the cruelest forms

of capital punishment ever devised. The idea that Jesus would undergo such treatment, willingly, was beyond Satan's comprehension.

If you had been there on that hill during these events, and looked at Jesus dying a horrible death on the cross, would you have thought that the plan was on track; Satan's plan, maybe, but God's plan to establish an earthly kingdom? I don't think so.

So, as Jesus said, **"My God, my God, why have you forsaken me?"** and then died, Satan would have been jumping for joy. He had thought that Jesus has been forsaken by God! But, Jesus wasn't asking a question of God, he was just quoting Scripture. The Scripture that he quoted was the twenty-second Psalm which describes the crucifixion. At this point Satan took Jesus in death and brought him to the lower regions, that is, hell.

I imagine that Satan at this point was peeing in his pants with excitement. To defeat Jesus was to win the game! What bliss! What bliss! Whatever God's plan was, it was clear to Satan that the plan had failed. Or, so Satan thought.

Luke 20:14–15
"But when the tenants saw him, they talked the matter over. 'This is the heir,' they said. 'Let's kill him, and the inheritance will be ours.' ¹⁵ So they threw him out of the vineyard and killed him. (NIV84)

This is a part of one of Jesus' parables. The tenants are Satan's people and are therefore speaking Satan's thoughts. Satan saw that Jesus was the heir of the earth, that is, God's Chosen One, and he figured that if he killed him that the earth would forever be his to do with as he chose. The vineyard in this case is symbolic of Jerusalem and this refers to the fact that Jesus was taken outside of the city and killed there.

Satan had his plan, but, God's plan can never fail. If God says it, it will happen. It is impossible for even one word of God's to fall to the ground. Jesus was in hell, yes, but illegally. He had never committed sin. The sin that was on him was, more or less, a costume. Death could not hold Jesus. Therefore, death had no dominion over Jesus and could not hold him. Jesus then burst out of Hell and was resurrected.

Revelation 1:18
I am the Living One; I was dead, and behold I am alive for ever and ever! And I hold the keys of death and Hades.
(NIV84)

Before the crucifixion/resurrection there was no path from death to life.

While you lived in this world you could continue to live in the flesh, but when your body died your spirit could not go to live with God. This was because each and every soul was guilty of sin. Man was doomed; destined to be denied life with God. And there was absolutely nothing that man could do about it, because every man was guilty of sin against God. Satan was all too eager to point out this fact, and the sins of guilty man.

I want to step back a moment here and explain something about the earth, that is, the physical creation. Satan and his angels could not legally live in heaven after they sinned, and they did not have the power, wisdom and understanding to create an existence for themselves, any more than man does. Think about this a minute. If you can't live in heaven with God, and you can't create another place to live, then you must live in some formless void. That was Satan's dilemma. But then God created the earth and Satan saw his opportunity. Satan saw the earth as a place in which he could live and not just live, but rule. He wanted the earth for himself and so he did what he did. Satan succeeded with his plan and he became the god of this world, so to say.

But then God sent another Adam, that is, another sinless man, Jesus Christ (his own Son) to take the earth away from Satan. Satan was understandably worried and threatened. Satan set up his own plan; a plan to capture Jesus in sin and get him under his own control, just as he did with the first Adam. Jesus fell right into Satan's plan and died on the cross and was buried in the earth, by the hand of Satan. But then, the unexpected occurred, Jesus then threw off death and ascended up out of Hell into a resurrected life because of his actual sinless life. Satan lost control of Jesus, but what did it mean? Satan didn't understand any of this, any more than the people of that day did, or this day to tell the truth.

It is fine for Jesus to defeat death, but how could that help man? How is it possible for sinful man to benefit from this sacrifice that Jesus participated in? Well, it is a matter of faith and marriage. That's right, faith and marriage.

When I say faith here, I am not talking about a religious experience; I am talking about an understanding of the possibility of a relationship with God, and of a belief that God has made that possibility possible through Jesus Christ. Look at this example from the book of Acts. In this story we see that Cornelius, a Gentile that believed in the God of Abraham, Isaac and Jacob, was visited by an angel that told him to send for the apostle Peter, so that Peter would tell him things about God. This man and his

extended family believed in God, they knew that Jesus was a holy man that had been faithful in doing Gods will, but did not understand what Jesus did through the cross. What Peter says in verse 43 triggers a belief on the part of the listening Gentiles. Verse 43 contains what these believers lacked to become born-again believers.

> **Acts 10:34–46**
> **Then Peter began to speak: "I now realize how true it is that God does not show favoritism [35] but accepts men from every nation who fear him and do what is right. [36] You know the message God sent to the people of Israel, telling the good news of peace through Jesus Christ, who is Lord of all. [37] You know what has happened throughout Judea, beginning in Galilee after the baptism that John preached— [38] how God anointed Jesus of Nazareth with the Holy Spirit and power, and how he went around doing good and healing all who were under the power of the devil, because God was with him.**
> **[39] "We are witnesses of everything he did in the country of the Jews and in Jerusalem. They killed him by hanging him on a tree, [40] but God raised him from the dead on the third day and caused him to be seen. [41] He was not seen by all the people, but by witnesses whom God had already chosen— by us who ate and drank with him after he rose from the dead. [42] He commanded us to preach to the people and to testify that he is the one whom God appointed as judge of the living and the dead. [43] *All the prophets testify about him that everyone who believes in him receives forgiveness of sins through his name."***
> **[44] While Peter was still speaking these words, the Holy Spirit came on all who heard the message. [45] The circumcised believers who had come with Peter were astonished that the gift of the Holy Spirit had been poured out even on the Gentiles. [46] For they heard them speaking in tongues and praising God. (NIV84)**

Before Peter spoke to them they fully believed in God. What they didn't know, deep down in their spirit natures, was that they could be made spiritually clean through Jesus Christ, and so be accepted by God. Jesus had defeated the Devil, but unless you know this, and unless you believe that this fact has something to do with you, you cannot have faith for salvation.

I will give you an example of what I mean. Suppose you have met the love of your life, your soulmate as it were, but you feel down in the core of your being that you are not good enough for him or her, what then?

Suppose that this 'soulmate' is beautiful/handsome beyond words and is wealthy beyond counting and has many other 'beautiful people' running after him or her. How can you hope for this person, that you are so unworthy of? You know, you totally know, that you are not the person that this loved-one deserves. You know that you are a stupid person and are basically clueless and by comparison you are destitute; can you really expect this other person to love you after they really know you? Once they know you, will they really want to be married to you? Isn't it a certainty that you will be rejected only moments after you introduce yourself?

This is, more or less, you and God. God is so perfect, so holy and pure, so powerful and worthy, but who are you to presume anything with God? What could God do to convince you of his true love for you?

Cornelius showed by his previous actions that he loved God, but he did not know that God loved him in return and that God had spiritually cleaned him so that he was now be pure as snow. Cornelius did not know that God had already made him, on the inside, holy and pure, acceptable to God. When Peter, a man that Cornelius knew had been sent from God to inform him of a very important truth concerning God, told him that Jesus Christ made it possible that our sins to be completely and forever removed from us, he then dared to hope, that is, he had faith that God would receive him, and so he reached out in faith, reached out from his heart, and was received by God in a holy union. God confirmed the holy union between himself and Cornelius, and with those who had faith along with Cornelius, by uniting with them all in their hearts—Spirit to spirit—and gave the sign of his acceptance of the Gentile believers to Peter by having the Gentile believers speak in tongues. The sign of tongues was for Peter and not for Cornelius and his family. Cornelius had a full testimony of God's acceptance within him, but Peter could not know that, so the sign of tongues was for Peter and the Jews.

God cannot live in a sinful heart. The fact that he bonded with the believers—Spirit to spirit—is confirmation that in their spirit natures had been cleaned. All of this concerning life and death and a possible relationship with God is about your spirit person, the spirit person that lives inside of you, and not about your mind and body. Your body along with its brain and mind are still separated from God. The union with God that is possible is the union of spirits and not a union of flesh. When you marry a man or a woman, that union is a union of the flesh. A man and a woman come together, through the act of sexual intercourse, to form

a single person of flesh.

1 Corinthians 6:16–17
Do you not know that he who unites himself with a pros-titute is one with her in body? For it is said, "The two will become one flesh." ¹⁷ But he who unites himself with the Lord is one with him in spirit. (NIV84)

A husband and wife are no longer two physical people; they are one in much the same way that God is one. The union that they formed is one of flesh and was created because of a fleshly union, but the union that God makes with us is a union of spirit as it is by his spirit entering into us that they union is formed.

John 3:5–8
Jesus answered, "I tell you the truth, no one can enter the kingdom of God unless he is born of water and the Spirit. ⁶ Flesh gives birth to flesh, but the Spirit gives birth to spirit. ⁷ You should not be surprised at my saying, 'You must be born again.' ⁸ The wind blows wherever it pleases. You hear its sound, but you cannot tell where it comes from or where it is going. So it is with everyone born of the Spirit." (NIV84)

"**Flesh gives birth to flesh**" (the human baby, and the physical husband/wife); "**the Spirit gives birth to spirit**" (your inner spirit person which has been cut off from God and is therefore dead, has been reborn into a new life through the union with Christ's spirit). The first birth is carnal and is temporary, but the second birth, or rebirth, is spiritual and is eternal.

How does one become a partaker of the spiritual rebirth experience, through the marriage-like union with Jesus Christ, the bridegroom? Jesus accomplishes the defeat of death by taking from Satan the keys to death and hell, and then proposes to us and declares to us his love for us by his willingness to die for us. Jesus had no need of defeating death for himself. He was never subject to death. He willingly and obediently subjected himself to death for us who were under death's power.

Isaiah 53:5
But he was pierced for our transgressions, he was crushed for our iniquities; the punishment that brought us peace was upon him, and by his wounds we are healed. (NIV84)

Romans 5:6–8
You see, at just the right time, when we were still power-less, Christ died for the ungodly. ⁷ Very rarely will anyone die for a righteous man, though for a good man someone might possibly dare to die. ⁸ But God demonstrates his own

love for us in this: While we were still sinners, Christ died for us. (NIV84)

You have to think about all of this my friend. You should ask yourself, why did Christ die? Why was the plan for this from the beginning?

The spiritual union that the Bible talks about is a spiritual union whereby the male (God) enters into the female (man) with his spirit and this forms a spiritual union where the two become one spirit, that is, you thereafter exist inside of God and God surrounds you.

This marriage-like union that Jesus Christ made possible is a union of faith, which when you think about it is also true of human marriages. In our faithless world today marriage has lost much of its spiritual meaning. Sex today is not so much as an act that produces births, but is a physical pleasure of the body much like taking drugs. People today talk of sex addictions, birth control, one night stands, sport sex and who knows what all.

It is through our obedience to the Bible's instruction (what the world calls being moral) that we gain understanding of spiritual matters. What does consensual sex between adults have to do with morality? We observe instructions from God on matters of sex in order to understand how and why a spiritual union with Jesus Christ does what it does. In fact, every instruction from God is there to show us something very important concerning a possible relationship with God.

A person obeys God because they understand that through their obedience they will be drawn closer to God. A person obeys God also because they care about the other person. By this I mean that if I truly love someone else then I will do to them, or for them, whatever is best for them. I will not have sex with another man's wife not only because of what such an act would do to me, but also because of what it would do to her. In fact, if I am filled with divine love then that love will protect her, and only as a secondary effect, protect me.

Looking back at what I said earlier concerning Jesus Christ and what he did and how that helps us, we can now see that as Jesus is resurrected from death to life, we die to the world and take Jesus up on his offer of marriage to us. Do you remember that I said that this was a matter of faith and marriage? Well the union is a marriage-like union (of spirit and not of flesh) that is accomplished through faith. Jesus says, "I love you so much that I will suffer death for you. Will you abandon sin and live for God? Will you unite to me as my bride and obey me as your husband?

Will you be one with me in spirit as I am one with God?"

In order to be united to Christ you must have faith. You must believe that all of this happened just as the Bible says that it did. Jesus came to the earth to reveal the Father to us and he endured the cross to provide a way for us to be reunited to God through him. What are you going to do about this?

Can you see that this has nothing to do with religion? We either become Christ's bride or we do not. We either desire to escape the world's way of life and enter into a life of love and hope and faith, or we remain in the world, living as the world lives. If we choose Christ then we become like him in his spirit and as such we take control of our bodies and make them obedient to us. Jesus made his body completely obedient to him, that is, to the will of the Father and so we, when we become like him, do the same thing.

> **Philippians 2:5–11**
> **Your attitude should be the same as that of Christ Jesus:**
> **⁶ Who, being in very nature God, did not consider equality with God something to be grasped, ⁷ but made himself nothing, taking the very nature of a servant, being made in human likeness. ⁸ And being found in appearance as a man, he humbled himself and became obedient to death— even death on a cross! ⁹ Therefore God exalted him to the highest place and gave him the name that is above every name, ¹⁰ that at the name of Jesus every knee should bow, in heaven and on earth and under the earth, ¹¹ and every tongue confess that Jesus Christ is Lord, to the glory of God the Father.** (NIV84)

We are told to be like Jesus, that is, to be obedient and humble like him. This passage tells us that because of Jesus' obedience and humility that God exalted him to the highest possible place and put everything else under his authority. We are told to be like this too. Through our understanding of what happened and why it happened and that we understand that God will extend to us his very self if we will just believe in what he did, that is, have faith in him, we too can share in Jesus' resurrection. We who are dead because of sin can be metaphorically buried in baptism and subsequently resurrected to new live in Christ Jesus.

The thing about faith is that it must be real and true. There can be no doubt or it is not faith. Another thing about faith is that it cannot be manufactured or wished or hoped for and wanted badly enough. You must

have complete faith or you have no faith. That is the way it works. I don't mean that you must understand everything. I mean that you understand the birth, obedience, death and resurrection of Christ and of his offer to you. Understand that much and then follow him. As you walk with Christ in this capacity you will then understand more and more. Be faithful to what you know.

An act of unfaithfulness is virtually unrepairable. If your spouse cheats on you and you find out about it, what can he or she do to restore a state of holy and pure faith again? If you cheat on your spouse what can you do to convince him or her that you are completely faithful? If you truly do repent and are totally faithful again, can you really, totally, unreservedly, believe that your spouse has completely forgiven you and has accepted your declaration of faith without reservation. You see, with God it is all or nothing. Faith is a total thing; otherwise it would not be faith. But this doesn't mean that we who come to Christ are perfect, far from it. We all stumble, but we get back up and trudge along again. We never, ever, give up. As the Bible says, the spirit is willing but the flesh is weak. In our hearts we hate the deeds of our flesh. Our flesh wants this and it wants that, but we grab hold of it and never stop trying to control it.

We can say that in the Garden man had a baby bond of faith, but now we can have an adult bond of faith that is possible because we now know Good and Evil and can see that Good is better than Evil and so we, of our own free will, can choose an everlasting relationship with the God of Correctness.

Luke 7:36–50
Now one of the Pharisees invited Jesus to have dinner with him, so he went to the Pharisee's house and reclined at the table. ³⁷ When a woman who had lived a sinful life in that town learned that Jesus was eating at the Pharisee's house, she brought an alabaster jar of perfume, ³⁸ and as she stood behind him at his feet weeping, she began to wet his feet with her tears. Then she wiped them with her hair, kissed them and poured perfume on them.
³⁹ When the Pharisee who had invited him saw this, he said to himself, "If this man were a prophet, he would know who is touching him and what kind of woman she is—that she is a sinner."
⁴⁰ Jesus answered him, "Simon, I have something to tell you."
"Tell me, teacher," he said.
⁴¹ "Two men owed money to a certain moneylender. One

owed him five hundred denarii, and the other fifty. [42] Neither of them had the money to pay him back, so he canceled the debts of both. Now which of them will love him more?" [43] Simon replied, "I suppose the one who had the bigger debt canceled."

"You have judged correctly," Jesus said.

[44] Then he turned toward the woman and said to Simon, "Do you see this woman? I came into your house. You did not give me any water for my feet, but she wet my feet with her tears and wiped them with her hair. [45] You did not give me a kiss, but this woman, from the time I entered, has not stopped kissing my feet. [46] You did not put oil on my head, but she has poured perfume on my feet. [47] Therefore, I tell you, her many sins have been forgiven—for she loved much. But he who has been forgiven little loves little."

[48] Then Jesus said to her, "Your sins are forgiven."

[49] The other guests began to say among themselves, "Who is this who even forgives sins?"

[50] Jesus said to the woman, "Your faith has saved you; go in peace." (NIV84)

We, those that see the forgiving path of God, are like this woman. We have been lost in sin and there has been no path back to righteousness. But when we see the path, we drop everything and we weep for joy at our restoration, our adoption back into the blessed family of God. As the song goes,

Amazing Grace

Amazing grace how sweet the sound,
that saved a wretch like me.
I was lost but now I'm found,
was lost but now I see.

T'was Grace that taught...
my heart to fear.
And Grace, my fears relieved.
How precious did that Grace appear...
the hour I first believed.

Through many dangers, toils and snares...
we have already come.
T'was Grace that brought us safe thus far...
and Grace will lead us home.

The Lord has promised good to me ...
His word my hope secures.
He will my shield and portion be ...
as long as life endures.

Yea, when this flesh and heart shall fail,
And mortal life shall cease,
I shall possess within the veil,
a life of joy and peace.

When we've been here ten thousand years...
bright shining as the sun.
We've no less days to sing God's praise...
then when we've first begun.

Amazing grace how sweet the sound,
that saved a wretch like me.
I was lost but now I'm found,
was lost but now I see.

That song is Scripture as far as I am concerned. It so perfectly expresses the truth concerning our being led away into sin and our seeing salvation in Christ.

There is another reason that Jesus came in the flesh and that is to serve as an example for us. This is not just an academic truth. If we aspire to be received by God into his household it behooves us to clean up our act so that we will easily integrate into his family.

Jesus serves us as an example of a man that lives life in a way that is pleasing to God.

Matthew 3:17
And a voice from heaven said, "This is my Son, whom I love; with him I am well pleased." (NIV84)

We who have been living within the sinful world for many years and have been raised in its evil ways may find it difficult to throw off the old and live in the new, but we must, to the limit of our abilities try and do just that. Growth doesn't happen overnight, but things that are alive grow and we must be growing into godliness. Those that are saved are saved from death into life. If we were once dead then we need to grow in our life to become honorable sons and daughters of the Lord God Almighty.

Matthew 22:11–14
"But when the king came in to see the guests, he noticed a man there who was not wearing wedding clothes. [12] 'Friend,' he asked, 'how did you get in here without wedding clothes?' The man was speechless.
[13] "Then the king told the attendants, 'Tie him hand and foot, and throw him outside, into the darkness,
where there will be weeping and gnashing of teeth.'
[14] "For many are invited, but few are chosen." (NIV84)

Destiny

Chapter Sixteen

E HAVE SEEN BEFORE THAT Jesus said that not one word, not the smallest letter, not one stroke of the pen, will disappear from the Scriptures until everything that they say has been fulfilled. [1]

Therefore, we can clearly see that the world is completely destined to go the way that it is destined to go. There is nothing, and I mean nothing, that you or I or anyone can do to change that. So, we can say that destiny is a fact.

What of your destiny? Is that forgone too? Are you destined to live and die according to a plan set down before the world was?

Ephesians 1:11–12
In him we were also chosen, having been predestined according to the plan of him who works out everything in conformity with the purpose of his will, [12] in order that we, who were the first to hope in Christ, might be for the praise of his glory. (NIV84)

The above passage might seem like it says that you were predestined to be in Christ, but that is not what it is actually saying. Some people were predestined to be in Christ, but the actual persons were not. God knew that when he provided salvation through Jesus Christ that some people would believe it and respond and that others would not. But, I don't

---

1) Matthew 5:17-18

want you to get the idea that things are left to chance. Chance plays no part in it whatsoever. God is actively working at all times and in every circumstance to bring about the exact plan that he worked out before time began. You are a person that lives in the world and as such you are carried along the stream of humanity but your personal place in things is not totally set. What I mean is that if the stream of humanity is picking up speed and headed for the rapids you will be affected, but your place with God is not necessarily affected. You will enter into the rapids along with everyone else, but what happens to you is not predestined. Some will come to harm in the rapids, but not necessarily you. Some will be strengthened, but not necessarily you.

Humanity is predestined, but all of the individuals are not. If you are reading this then you have choices that you can make. You can affect the outcome of your life. If you can see the light, then embrace the light. If you can hear the call, then respond to the call.

The plan of God is marching on and will continue to march along its exact path; get on board with God.

I don't want you to think that what you do does not matter. What you do does matter; it matters to you and it matters to those that are affected by you. If you listen to God and obey him and in this way change yourself, this will affect everyone that is close to you. If you chose to drink yourself silly and be a total jerk, that will affect everyone around you as well.

Why are there prophecies in the Bible? If you stop and think about this question you will see that it is a good question and an interesting question. I haven't worked out all of the reasons but I will share with you some of my observations and thoughts on the matter.

To God the history of the world is already done. From the very beginning until the very end of the universe every event is complete. The Bible records every major point of God's plan so that we can not only see what has happened from the beginning of time, but also everything that happens before the end. If you want to know what the effect of sin is, then read the Bible and be enlightened. If you want to know what is going on in the world today and why, then read the Bible and see.

What did Satan and the fallen angels do? What happened to them and why? What will happen to them because of their rebellion? All of this can be seen by you and understood, if you have the heart to find out.

The Bible is a compete history of the world and that is because of

prophecy. Prophecy, by the way, is not only a foretelling of what is to come, it can also a telling of what has happened in the past. Prophecy is the speaking of God's words. If God uses someone to speak his words then those words are prophecy. This is true if the words concern the distant past, the recent past, the present, or any part of the future. If God is speaking through a person, even if that person doesn't know it, it is prophecy. The whole Bible, from the beginning to the end is prophecy.

I would say that one of the primary purposes of prophecy is to inform us as to what is going on and why. Another purpose of the prophecies is that they serve as a proof concerning the perfection and reliability of the Bible. When God foretells of some unexpected event and then the event comes to pass, we are then assured that everything else that the Bible is talking about is true too. So, foretelling the future is proof that God is God.

Isaiah 44:7
Who then is like me? Let him proclaim it. Let him declare and lay out before me what has happened since I estab-lished my ancient people, and what is yet to come— yes, let him foretell what will come. (NIV84)

Notice that this passage challenges man to show some other force or being that can accurately foretell the future and the long lost past. God is saying that he can and because of that he is God. God's prophecies are very detailed and exact. When they are being fulfilled there can be no doubt.

Isaiah 44:8
Do not tremble, do not be afraid. Did I not proclaim this and foretell it long ago? You are my witnesses. Is there any God besides me? No, there is no other Rock; I know not one." (NIV84)

This is the next passage from the above prophecy in Isaiah. It tells us another reason for the prophecies. They give comfort in frightening times. When we are trusting in the Lord and the world sails into troubled waters we can rest in the knowledge that whatever has come upon the world is not unexpected. God is in charge and he will bring his children through it, one way or the other.

My friends, the world is headed toward a time of massive scary. Within a very short time billions of people are going to die. Everyone will be frightened, but those that know what is going on will have some peace because they know that this is what God foretold. They will also be able to rest in the understanding that because they are finding themselves within

all of this destruction that that doesn't mean that they are doomed. God forewarned us that those believers that are alive at the time when all of this goes down will still be his children and that God will still fulfill every promise to them. If you don't know this you might become dismayed and lose hope and faith.

Isaiah 46:10–11
I make known the end from the beginning, from ancient times, what is still to come. I say: My purpose will stand, and I will do all that I please. [11] From the east I summon a bird of prey; from a far-off land, a man to fulfill my purpose. What I have said, that will I bring about; what I have planned, that will I do. (NIV84)

God has made it clear that there is no possibility of his plan not occurring exactly has he has determined it.

Job 42:2
"I know that you can do all things; no plan of yours can be thwarted. (NIV84)

So, God's plan is set in stone, so to say, what can you or I do about it? We cannot change the plan, so we had better get on board; don't you think?

I like to think of God's plan as sort of like screenplay that has already been written by God and written down for us to read. God wrote it down so that we can know what is happening and why. We don't have to be surprised or overly frightened. We know that our Father is in control.

God is looking for players to play the roles. The roles will be filled by someone, including you and me, but it has not been determine which roles you or I must play. We are given the opportunity to make ourselves ready for whatever role we wish to have, but God is the Producer and the Director and he will cast the parts as he determines best. So, therefore, it behooves us to makes ourselves as ready as possible for the roles that bring a blessing and not be cast as in the roles that result in destruction. I am very serious here.

2 Timothy 2:20–21
In a large house there are articles not only of gold and silver, but also of wood and clay; some are for noble purposes and some for ignoble. 21 If a man cleanses himself from the latter, he will be an instrument for noble purposes, made holy, useful to the Master and prepared to do any good work. (NIV84)

You should spend some time thinking about the meaning of the above passage. What does it mean to cleanse yourself from the ignoble so that you might be useful to the Master for noble purposes? Do you want to play the role of an apostle? Do you want to play the role of a teacher? A prophet? An evangelist? A servant of God? A child of God? Which role do you want for yourself? Prepare for that role.

1 Corinthians 9:24–27
Do you not know that in a race all the runners run, but only one gets the prize? Run in such a way as to get the prize. ²⁵ Everyone who competes in the games goes into strict training. They do it to get a crown that will not last; but we do it to get a crown that will last forever. ²⁶ Therefore I do not run like a man running aimlessly; I do not fight like a man beating the air. ²⁷ No, I beat my body and make it my slave so that after I have preached to others, I myself will not be disqualified for the prize. (NIV84)

Does this passage say it all or what? These are the words of Paul, a man that wanted to fulfill the role of a man that was very useful to God. Paul wanted this and he devoted his life to this end. Paul was a driven man that drove himself to a life of discipline and effective works.

Years ago there was a rock opera titled Jesus Christ Superstar and one of the songs (The Last Supper) had a line that said, Always hoped that I'd be an apostle/ Knew that I would make it if I tried … When I heard that song I wasn't a believer, but something about that song and that album played on my mind. Later, when I had become a believer, that song came back to me and motivated me to keep reading the Bible. I wanted to be an apostle. I am not an apostle, but I had been motivated nonetheless, and still today I work toward improving myself in the eyes of God, so that God can use me for good works. My friends, you have a role to play in all of this. The plan is set, yes, but your personal destiny is not set. God has set before you options.

Deuteronomy 30:11–16
Now what I am commanding you today is not too difficult for you or beyond your reach. ¹² It is not up in heaven, so that you have to ask, "Who will ascend into heaven to get it and proclaim it to us so we may obey it?" ¹³ Nor is it beyond the sea, so that you have to ask, "Who will cross the sea to get it and proclaim it to us so we may obey it?" ¹⁴ No, the word is very near you; it is in your mouth and in your heart so you may obey it. ¹⁵ See, I set before you today life and prosperity, death and destruction. ¹⁶ For I command you today to love

the Lord your God, to walk in his ways, and to keep his commands, decrees and laws; then you will live and increase, and the Lord your God will bless you in the land you are entering to possess. (NIV84)

Believers in the World

Chapter Seventeen

In a Nutshell

*W*E NEED TO BACK UP and look that the whole situation. God created the whole world and put perfect man on it. Everything was perfect. Everything was perfect until man broke faith with God, in a way that was very much like what the angels did, and then man, cut off from God as he was, was more or less controlled by his natural human instincts, and because spiritual man was hidden within his physical body, he was vulnerable to spiritual attack from spiritual beings more knowledgeable than he was. God then promised a savior for man, and told man that if man would live by faith in God and in his coming savior that he would be spiritually protected in the world. Man, however, could not, or would not, perceive his weakness in a spiritual world and became proud and self-seeking—the very worst of things, and so he became prey to spiritual forces stronger than he.

Genesis 6:5–8
The Lord saw how great man's wickedness on the earth had become, and that every inclination of the thoughts of his heart was only evil all the time. ⁶ The Lord was grieved that he had made man on the earth, and his heart was filled with pain. ⁷ So the Lord said, "I will wipe mankind, whom I

have created, from the face of the earth—men and animals, and creatures that move along the ground, and birds of the air—for I am grieved that I have made them." [8] But Noah found favor in the eyes of the Lord. (NIV84)

Please don't think that what you think of as evil is the same as what God thinks of as evil. Many if not most of the people today in the world are every bit as evil as those that this passage is talking about.

That sums up the first round. God makes man, man falls away and becomes evil, God destroys man. All this happened pretty quick, thereabouts 1500 years from Adam to Noah; quick, but also a pretty long time as history on the earth goes.

2 Peter 3:5–7
But they deliberately forget that long ago by God's word the heavens existed and the earth was formed out of water and by water. [6] By these waters also the world of that time was deluged and destroyed. [7] By the same word the present heavens and earth are reserved for fire, being kept for the day of judgment and destruction of ungodly men. (NIV84)

We see in Peter's statement that the flood was a shadow of the events that will soon come upon the earth. Understand this: if God destroyed that world because the people were evil, the destruction that is soon coming is because the people are again evil, to the core. God would not destroy the world if it were not evil.

Before the flood people had no history from which to learn from. They did not understand the consequences of deliberate disobedience. But after the flood we have a record of what happened and why. Man now knows, that if the world becomes totally wicked, that God will destroy it. We have been warned.

Something that is very important to understand in this is that even though almost every man, woman and child was wicked, God saved Noah and his family because they were not wicked. Today there are a great many believers that live in the world. They have heeded the warning and truly fear God. God has a big stick and they know it. When the coming destruction comes, God will save his children, so that they will not be wiped away with all of the wicked and rebellious unbelievers. These stupid movies that depict the roving bands of evil and wicked people after the apocalypse are all total fantasy. When the destruction hits every single wicked fool will perish. That is the mathematics of the apocalypse. The world will be wiped clean for the righteous to inherit.

Matthew 24:37
As it was in the days of Noah, so it will be at the coming of the Son of Man. (NIV84)

Matthew 5:5
Blessed are the meek, for they will inherit the earth. (NIV84)

Should you be afraid, yes, if you are rebellious towards God. This judgment is coming and there is nothing that anyone, or everyone collectively, can do to stop or even delay it. Billions of people are soon going to die—billions. Who likes that? God doesn't like that, and man doesn't like it, and certainly doesn't like what is coming either. It is horrible and it is totally scary, but it is coming. It is coming because sin cannot be controlled. Sin is like a raging fire that is ablaze within the dry forest—out of control and hell bent.

In the days of Noah sin ran rampant and there was nothing to slow it down. But after the days of Noah we had the testimony of Noah and his family to inform us as to the price of sin.

Instructing Man

SOMETIME AFTER THE DAYS OF Noah, thereabouts 300 years after, God raised up a man that would walk with him. That man was Abram, later named Abraham. Next to Jesus, Abraham is the most important man that has ever lived. God took that one insignificant man and formed from him a people for himself. People today usually call Abraham's descendants Jews, but I like to call them the children of Israel, because to my mind this name is really a more accurate name.

The point here is that Abraham had a relationship with God Almighty. Abraham's son Isaac also had a relationship with God and one of Isaac's sons, Jacob also had a relationship with the Lord God.

When Abraham was an old man God had made a deal him, or said in biblical language, God man a covenant with Abraham.

Genesis 17:1–14
When Abram was ninety-nine years old, the Lord appeared to him and said, "I am God Almighty; walk before me and be blameless. ² I will confirm my covenant between me and you and will greatly increase your numbers."
³ Abram fell facedown, and God said to him, 4 "As for me, this is my covenant with you: You will be the father of many nations. ⁵ No longer will you be called Abram; your name will be Abraham, for I have made you a father of many na-

tions. ⁶ I will make you very fruitful; I will make nations of you, and kings will come from you. ⁷ I will establish my covenant as an everlasting covenant between me and you and your descendants after you for the generations to come, to be your God and the God of your descendants after you. ⁸ The whole land of Canaan, where you are now an alien, I will give as an everlasting possession to you and your descendants after you; and I will be their God."

⁹ Then God said to Abraham, "As for you, you must keep my covenant, you and your descendants after you for the generations to come. ¹⁰ This is my covenant with you and your descendants after you, the covenant you are to keep: Every male among you shall be circumcised. ¹¹ You are to undergo circumcision, and it will be the sign of the covenant between me and you. ¹² For the generations to come every male among you who is eight days old must be circumcised, including those born in your household or bought with money from a foreigner—those who are not your offspring. ¹³ Whether born in your household or bought with your money, they must be circumcised. My covenant in your flesh is to be an everlasting covenant. ¹⁴ Any uncircumcised male, who has not been circumcised in the flesh, will be cut off from his people; he has broken my covenant." (NIV84)

This is a pivotal point in the history of mankind. Again, apart from Jesus' birth-life-death-resurrection, this is the most important event in the history of man. God promised a relationship with those that were a part of this covenant, not only with Abraham's descendants but with all those peoples of the nations that would believe in God through this covenant. If you are a Christian today it is through this covenant that you have your relationship with God. Wowie-zowie!

There is a subtle but important thing going on here that I want you to see. The promise of a relationship was made to Abraham and to Abraham's seed, who is Christ Jesus. There are two groups here: Abraham's physical descendants (the Jews) and to his Seed (Jesus). This can be a bit confusing because the Jews have a covenant with God and Jesus is the fulfillment of that same covenant, but the Jews can have a relationship with God because they are Jews, and have faith in God, and also because they are believers in Christ Jesus. Just because a Jew doesn't accept Christ at this time doesn't mean that they are not partakers of the covenant of Abraham. This is not true for the Gentile believers. The Gentiles, more or less, do not have a relationship with God unless it is through Jesus Christ. We will be looking into this a much more detail later, but for now

please understand that the Jews, that is, the children of Israel, the physical descendants of Abraham through Jacob, his grandson, have a valid covenant with God that, as the Bible says, can never be revoked. This is the covenant by virtue of their descent, and by virtue of circumcision. If a descendant of Abraham puts their faith in God though the covenant of circumcision they have a relationship with God, even if they are not partakers of the covenant of new-life in Christ through his resurrection.

> **Romans 11:25–32**
> **I do not want you to be ignorant of this mystery, brothers, so that you may not be conceited: Israel has experienced a hardening in part until the full number of the Gentiles has come in. ²⁶ And so all Israel will be saved, as it is written:**
> **"The deliverer will come from Zion;**
> **he will turn godlessness away from Jacob.**
> **²⁷ And this is my covenant with them**
> **when I take away their sins."**
> **²⁸ As far as the gospel is concerned, they are enemies on your account; but as far as election is concerned, they are loved on account of the patriarchs, ²⁹ for God's gifts and his call are irrevocable. ³⁰ Just as you who were at one time disobedient to God have now received mercy as a result of their disobedience, ³¹ so they too have now become disobedient in order that they too may now receive mercy as a result of God's mercy to you. ³² For God has bound all men over to disobedience so that he may have mercy on them all. (NIV84)**

The children of Israel are a people that are set apart from every other people in the world. They are the people of the Old Testament, almost exclusively, and they are the people of most of the prophecies of all ages. The children of Israel are the focus of almost all biblical prophecies relating to the end times. You must understand this fact to understand the prophecies. People have been trying to put the Church into the prophecies and the Church doesn't work. There are a few prophecies that relate to the Church but most do not. In the Old Testament the Church is almost completely invisible.

The people of Israel are sort of a teaching tool to the world to show the world what a relationship with God is all about. The Israelites are symbolic for all believers, that is, all people that have been called into a relationship with God.

It is very helpful to look at the meaning of the name Israel. Jacob was Abraham's grandson and he too had a relationship with God, however

Jacob's relationship was a little bit less harmonious with God than his father's or his grandfather's.

Genesis 32:24–30
So Jacob was left alone, and a man wrestled with him till daybreak. ²⁵ When the man saw that he could not overpower him, he touched the socket of Jacob's hip so that his hip was wrenched as he wrestled with the man. ²⁶ Then the man said, "Let me go, for it is daybreak."
But Jacob replied, "I will not let you go unless you bless me."
²⁷ The man asked him, "What is your name?"
"Jacob," he answered. ²⁸
Then the man said, "Your name will no longer be Jacob, but Israel, because you have struggled with God and with men and have overcome." ²⁹ Jacob said, "Please tell me your name."
But he replied, "Why do you ask my name?" Then he blessed him there.
³⁰ So Jacob called the place Peniel, saying, "It is because I saw God face to face, and yet my life was spared." (NIV84)

Jacob wrestled with God and lived. This is very interesting. The name Israel literally means One who has struggled with God and prevailed. The idea is that Jacob didn't have the smoothest relationship with God, but he did have a relationship, and it was a relationship where he remained with God no matter what. You can think in terms of a human marriage. If a marriage hits a rocky point and one of the parties calls it quit then the marriage did not prevail. But, if on the other hand, both parties stick to the marriage and the marriage survives, then you can say that the marriage prevailed. That is how it was with Israel. The union between God and Israel hit many rocky spots, but the relationship nonetheless prevailed.

When you look at the life of Jacob you can see that he pretty much didn't make any life changes unless he was forced into them. We can see that he knew that he should do something, but would not, until circumstances forced him to do it.

Genesis 31:10–13
"In breeding season I once had a dream in which I looked up and saw that the male goats mating with the flock were streaked, speckled or spotted. ¹¹ The angel of God said to me in the dream, 'Jacob.' I answered, 'Here I am.' ¹² And he said, 'Look up and see that all the male goats mating with the flock are streaked, speckled or spotted, for I have seen all that Laban has been doing to you. ¹³ I am the God of

Bethel, where you anointed a pillar and where you made a vow to me. Now leave this land at once and go back to your native land.' " (NIV84)

Notice that Jacob had been told to leave some time before, but he didn't go anywhere, not until he feared that Laban was going to come and do him harm. This is typical of his obedience. This is typical of anyone that has a struggling relationship with God. It is better to be quick to learn and quick to do that which you believe that the Lord has led you to do. Quick to obedience is good, and slow requires some goading on God's part, which is usually somewhat painful or scary.

Anyway, Jacob's relationship with God was/is somewhat rocky, but there exists a relationship nonetheless. It is better to have a stormy relationship with God than no relationship. When we see the history of the people of Israel and watch and listen to God talking to them we see that this is still a relationship. Israel may be stiff necked, but God will stay with Israel to the end and he will make Israel into the people he wants them to be, because Israel, for good or for ill, is God's chosen people. (I am not suggesting that there is any ill in the relationship with God, rather it may be a perceived ill on Israel's part because of all the pain that Israel must go through to get to the end. This pain, however, was never necessary. Had Israel obeyed God from the beginning then things would have gone very smoothly as they did with Abraham and Isaac before him.)

My friends, as believers in Jesus Christ, we still need to read the history of the Israeli people and learn that most of our own difficult times are the result of our struggling with God, struggling because our hearts are hard too. We need to listen to God and do what God says, regardless of the cost. The Lord God is always right. We must do what it right even if we suffer personal loss as a result. The idea here is that through our obedience we learn what it means to be godly. We will then truly understand. If we do not trust God to be right, then we are a faithless people. If we wait for God to force us then we will face scary times. Obedience is always the best policy.

What we see in the Bible, and in the world, is that the Israelites are God's set apart people, and that God is teaching them his ways. They are there for their own good, yes, but they are also there to show everyone in the world God's ways. Abraham was not only the father of the Israelites, but the father of everyone that would believe in God, through him and his covenant with God.

The World Gone Astray

SO, IN THE BIBLICAL STORY we see that the world went astray and only Noah and his family had retained a relationship with God. Everyone else, and I mean everyone, sought to satisfy their own desires. You must remember that the world belongs to God and God will do with it what he wants. God created the world for a reason, and only those that are with God, and in harmony with his plan, will come though the world to end up with God. Everyone else, that is, everyone else, will be eternally lost. From the time of the flood to this very day, everyone that did not develop a relationship with God before he or she physically died was, and or is, lost for all time with no hope of redemption.

That is the meaning of Noah and the Flood. If you do not heed the warning as Noah did, and follow his example, then you will be lost as all those of that day were lost. God caused the Bible to be written for a reason, and he sent his prophets for a reason, and he sent his only beloved Son for a reason too, and if you don't get on board with that reason, then you will be lost. It is not the good people that go to heaven, for there are no good people. The people that go to heaven to live with God are the same people that lived with God while they still lived in the world.

The end times are fast approaching. The world is ripe for the second judgment of the whole earth. The world thinks that it is righteous, but righteousness means being right with God. Only those that are right with God can possibly be righteous. The only way to be right with God is to obey God, that is, have a relationship with God. There are only two ways that you can have relationship with God and one is being a faithful Jew, and the other is believing in Jesus Christ the Son of God in a faithful way. The second is by far the best, but the first is a relationship. The first relationship is one that is a struggle, because God will not leave the Jews alone until they accept Jesus Christ as the one that has come. Until the Jews accept Jesus Christ they are disobedient. There are, however, a large group of Israelites that are obedient to God and are therefore holy, but have not put their faith in Jesus, but we will look at this group later in this book.

The Judgment that is soon coming upon the whole world is coming because the peoples of the world are not in harmony with God. Can a husband have faith relationship with a wife that is not faithful to him? Think about this my friends.

The Believers

IN THE WORLD TODAY THERE are those that truly believe in God. Remember that believing in God is not believing in his existence, but believing that every word that proceeds out of his mouth is right and gives life. To believe in God is to put your trust in him.

If you are a believer then what do you believe? Who do you believe in? Do you believe in God, the creator of heaven and earth, or in some vague wishy-washy doesn't care much about anything God?

My friends, God is passionate. He is totally passionate.

Revelation 3:14–22
"To the angel of the church in Laodicea write:
These are the words of the Amen, the faithful and true witness, the ruler of God's creation. [15] I know your deeds, that you are neither cold nor hot. I wish you were either one or the other! [16] So, because you are lukewarm—neither hot nor cold—I am about to spit you out of my mouth. [17] You say, 'I am rich; I have acquired wealth and do not need a thing.' But you do not realize that you are wretched, pitiful, poor, blind and naked. [18] I counsel you to buy from me gold refined in the fire, so you can become rich; and white clothes to wear, so you can cover your shameful nakedness; and salve to put on your eyes, so you can see.
[19] Those whom I love I rebuke and discipline. So be earnest, and repent. [20] Here I am! I stand at the door and knock. If anyone hears my voice and opens the door, I will come in and eat with him, and he with me.
[21] To him who overcomes, I will give the right to sit with me on my throne, just as I overcame and sat down with my Father on his throne. [22] He who has an ear, let him hear what the Spirit says to the churches." (NIV84)

Does this sound like an impassionate God to you? Do the actions that you know about sound like those of a God who doesn't care? My friends, God loves those that are his with a passionate and powerful love. He sent his Son Jesus to the earth to suffer at the hands of evil men for his beloved children.

The Promise to the Believers

GOD HAS PROMISED TO EVERY believer an eternal relationship with him in heaven. He made that promise in the Garden of Eden and has worked toward the fulfillment of it for 6000 years now.

Hebrews 6:13–20
**When God made his promise to Abraham, since there was
no one greater for him to swear by, he swore by himself, [14]
saying, "I will surely bless you and give you many descendants." [15] And so after waiting patiently, Abraham received
what was promised.
[16] Men swear by someone greater than themselves, and the
oath confirms what is said and puts an end to all argument.
[17] Because God wanted to make the unchanging nature of
his purpose very clear to the heirs of what was promised,
he confirmed it with an oath. [18] God did this so that, by two
unchangeable things in which it is impossible for God to lie,
we who have fled to take hold of the hope offered to us may
be greatly encouraged. [19] We have this hope as an anchor
for the soul, firm and secure. It enters the inner sanctuary
behind the curtain, [20] where Jesus, who went before us, has
entered on our behalf. He has become a high priest forever,
in the order of Melchizedek. (NIV84)**

We have this promise by two unchangeable things; one, God himself
made the promise of salvation himself; and two, it is impossible for God
to lie, so we know, know, that the promise of eternal life with God is sure.

The Believers Live in the World

S BELIEVERS IN JESUS CHRIST we have been born-again in our
hearts, that is, our spirit person is alive toward God. But, God did
not take us out of the world but rather he left us here for now, so that
we can learn and teach.

John 17:13–19
**"I am coming to you now, but I say these things while I am
still in the world, so that they may have the full measure
of my joy within them. [14] I have given them your word and
the world has hated them, for they are not of the world any
more than I am of the world. [15] My prayer is not that you
take them out of the world but that you protect them from
the evil one. [16] They are not of the world, even as I am not
of it. [17] Sanctify them by the truth; your word is truth. [18] As
you sent me into the world, I have sent them into the world.
[19] For them I sanctify myself, that they too may be truly
sanctified. (NIV84)**

These were the words of Jesus Christ spoken on the night that he was
betrayed and arrested. When he talks about sanctification he is talking
about our learning, when he talks about sending his brothers out into the

world, it is for them to learn and to teach.

The world is a hard place for God's children to live. His children are moral and the world is not. His children are born of God, that is, born again in divine-love but live in a world of self-centeredness. We are truly children of God, but we live in corrupted bodies, that want everything evil. On the one hand we want to live selfless lives before God, but on the other hand, we live in bodies that make selflessness impossible.

Romans 7:21–25
So I find this law at work: When I want to do good, evil is right there with me. ²² For in my inner being I delight in God's law; ²³ but I see another law at work in the members of my body, waging war against the law of my mind and making me a prisoner of the law of sin at work within my members. ²⁴ What a wretched man I am! Who will rescue me from this body of death? ²⁵ Thanks be to God—through Jesus Christ our Lord!
So then, I myself in my mind am a slave to God's law, but in the sinful nature a slave to the law of sin. (NIV84)

It is helpful to understand the dual nature that is our makeup. When we understand it, we can better understand why it is so difficult to always be doing the right thing.

It seems to me that abstinence is an easier thing to deal with than moderation. We live in bodies of moderation, but are called to abstinence. Inside we want to be perfect, outside we are battle weary soldiers. We must however press on to the finish. We must never give up the fight.

The world is headed to disaster, and we live in the world. That has to be a hard thing. We are flying in a sputtering plane, spiraling down to crash, but must keep ourselves under control and maintain faith, in the face of terrifying understandings. We see people that we care deeply about sticking their heads in the ground. We have children that do not know the Lord. We have spouses that are headed the wrong way. We live in a world where almost no one will listen to us, and yet we must maintain faith. Jesus told us to teach, but where are the students? It is hard, but we must go on. We must go on because there is no other path.

www.ingramcontent.com/pod-product-compliance
Lightning Source LLC
Chambersburg PA
CBHW020038040426

42331CB00030B/10